Create Your Own Future!

Lyle E. Schaller

Create Your Own Future!

Abingdon Press
Nashville

CREATE YOUR OWN FUTURE!

Library of Congress Cataloging-in-Publication Data

Schaller, Lyle E.
    Create your own future! / Lyle E. Schaller.
      p. cm.
    ISBN 0-687-09846-7 (alk. paper)
    1. Church management. 2. Church growth. I. Title.
  BV652.5.S315 1991
  254–dc20   90-19334

MANUFACTURED IN THE UNITED STATES OF AMERICA

To

Jacob Nathaniel

CONTENTS

INTRODUCTION *11*

CHAPTER ONE   Where and How Do We Intervene? *17*

Three Predictable Patterns *19*
Why Not the Board? *21*
Potential Points of Intervention *22*
What Are the Choices? *26*
Why? *26*
Summary *30*

CHAPTER TWO   Creating That Committee *31*

Participation or Performance? *37*
Informed or Uninformed Discussions? *38*
Who Should Not Be on It? *39*
Avoid Self-Defeating Behavior! *41*
Who Do You Want? *41*
Why Not a Representative Committee? *43*
Who Chooses Them? *45*
The Greatest Danger *46*

CHAPTER THREE   What Are Reasonable Expectations? ... *48*

Grand Design or Single Issue? *53*
Incremental Change or Magic Bullet? *55*
Exceptions and Fringe Benefits *56*

CHAPTER FOUR   Choosing a Beginning Point 58

Six Common Beginning Points *58*
The Healthy Congregation *61*
Counting Is a Prerequisite to Planning *68*
What Is Our Niche? *71*
Two Beginning Points for Growth *73*
Reversing the Decline in the Large Church *75*
Looking at Entry Points *78*
What Can Happen? *79*

CHAPTER FIVE   The Quest for Quality 82

Age or Generation? *83*
What Is Acceptable Today? *85*

CHAPTER SIX   Reading the Election Returns 96

Can This Be a Useful Beginning Point? *99*

CHAPTER SEVEN   Carving Out a Niche 102

The Importance of That Third Place *103*
To Do or to Be? *105*
Eight Influential Changes *106*
What Does This Mean? *108*
Seven Alternatives *110*
What Is Our Niche? *112*
What Are the Possibilities? *113*

CHAPTER EIGHT   What Does It Cost to Go to Church? .. 116

Measuring Unit Costs *117*
Where Does It Go? *118*
Another Potential Beginning Point *120*
Up or Down? *121*
What Are the Variables? *123*

CHAPTER NINE   Tradition or Market? 125

A Useful Beginning Point *129*
That Market-Driven Minority *130*
Two Questions for Your Committee *132*

CHAPTER TEN   No Surprises! 134

What Are Your Assumptions? *135*

CHAPTER ELEVEN To Study or to Act? *138*

    Five Choices *139*
    The Best Choice *141*

CHAPTER TWELVE Implementing the Plan *144*

    What Happens Next? *145*
    What Did They Do? *147*
    The Influence of Momentum *150*
    Overcoming Resistance *151*

NOTES *153*

INTRODUCTION

DO PROTESTANT CONGREGATIONS PASS THROUGH A LIFE CYCLE that resembles the birth-to-death cycle of human beings? That was a popular frame of reference for looking at churches back in the 1950s and 1960s. This perspective suggested that new congregations were small, fragile, and dependent creations that resembled babies. As the years passed, these new missions grew in size and gradually became independent. As vigorous, future-oriented, active, and growing congregations, they resembled adults in their younger years. Eventually they plateaued in size and after several decades they naturally tended to shrink in numbers, to become increasingly past-oriented, to become less active, and to display a high degree of self-centeredness. Finally, the day would arrive when that congregation would disappear from the scene.

This scenario was reinforced by several mainline denominations who organized new churches every year to replace those that dissolved. The rough rule-of-thumb was and is two new congregations must be organized to produce a net gain of one. The parallel is that while approximately four million babies are born every year in the United States, that produces a net growth of less than two million in the total population because of the death of over two million Americans every year. An interesting contemporary coincidence is that in the average year 0.8 percent of the American population will die while 0.8 percent of the approximately 350,000 Protestant congregations in the United States also will cease to exist. The life expectancy of both human beings and Protestant congregations has increased greatly since the 1880s.

This life-cycle analogy was reinforced by various articles that appeared in religious periodicals suggesting how to plan a meaningful memorial service for the last Sunday of a congregation's existence. More importantly, the life-cycle analogy also was reinforced by the histories of hundreds of churches that were born sometime between 1880 and 1925, peaked in size in the dozen years following World War II, and dissolved in the 1950s or 1960s.

Those who are adherents of the life-cycle theory will find little in this book to interest them since this author is not a supporter of that analogy.

A larger number of people are convinced that God has prepared a detailed plan for every one of His churches and there is little that mere human beings can do to alter that plan. The call to Christians is to be faithful and obedient, not to question the preordained destiny of their churches. At least a few of those who share this theological position contend that at best planning is interference with the power of the Holy Spirit and at worst a denial of that power. Those Christians also will find little to interest them in this book.

A third group of Christians believe that through His creation God gave human beings a remarkable degree of freedom. One facet of that freedom is that we are free to accept or to reject Jesus Christ as the Son of God and as our Savior. That gift of freedom also enables us to enjoy lives filled with choices.

That same gift of freedom also enables churches to make choices. A worshiping community is not bound by the same constraints of a life cycle that limits the choices available to mere human beings. The two-hundred-year-old congregation may include more people, offer a broader range of choices in response to the religious needs of people, and enjoy a greater degree of vitality than ever before in its history. Instead of concentrating on the design of a memorial service to mark its demise, the ninety-year-old parish is free to design and implement a construction program that will provide a new church home for the next half century or longer.

This book has been written for the Christians from this third group. These are the leaders who are convinced God has given to them the freedom to plan, with the guidance of the Holy Spirit, the future of that particular worshiping community. They can study, reflect, plan, articulate their dreams, formulate goals, and implement those plans. With God's help all things are possible.

It also should be added that this book will be of limited value in the pastor-run congregation where volunteer leaders are never involved in formulating policy or choosing from among alternative scenarios for the future or initiating changes.

The primary audiences for this book consist of three groups. The first is those congregational and denominational leaders who are convinced of the value of ad hoc study groups and long-range planning committees. The second, and the number-one audience, includes the people who serve as volunteers on these ad hoc committees. The third is the professional staff members, both lay and ordained, who work with long-range planning or futures committees.

The outline was conceptualized in sequential terms, probably as a result of the fact that this author grew up in what Neil Postman has described as "typographic America."[1] The first chapter begins with the basic assumption that most congregations prefer continuity to change and suggests several points of intervention for those who seek to challenge the status quo. The heart of this long chapter, however, is in the argument that ad hoc committees possess several advantages that are rare in standing committees. That may explain the need to create a long-range planning or futures committee. The value of ad hoc committees is a thread that runs the length of the entire book.

One of the three most influential decisions in this entire process is the choice of criteria to be used in selecting the members of this special committee. Suggestions for creating the committee are offered in the second chapter.

While rarely discussed in these terms, a second big fork in the road concerns the charge to the committee. Will it be expected to bring in recommendations designed to solve all problems? Or will it concentrate on a single issue? That choice is the theme of the third chapter.

The third of those three influential decisions in this entire process concerns the beginning point for the deliberations of that futures committee. In one sense this sets both the direction and the tone for all subsequent discussions by the long-range planning committee. The crucial importance of that decision on where to begin and suggestions on alternative beginning points is why that fourth chapter is so long.

The fifth chapter discusses one of the most significant changes in American Protestantism in this century. That is the demand by younger generations of churchgoers for a higher level of quality in all facets of congregational life. While this is a side trip from the basic sequence, the issue is one that cannot be ignored by long-range planning committees.

Two other approaches to that question of beginning points are examined in chapters 6 and 7. Another side trip is taken in the eighth chapter in a discussion of why the costs of going to church are rising faster than the increases in personal income. This chapter is of special significance to leaders in smaller churches and to denominational policy makers as well as to the members of the futures committee. The rising cost of fringe benefits, and especially health insurance, is pricing many smaller congregations out of the ministerial marketplace.

Three fork-in-the-road questions for the long-range planning committee are reviewed in chapters 9, 10, and 11. These often are overlapping concerns, especially if several of the recommendations will challenge sacred local traditions. This often means one of the tactical questions for the committee is when and how to build support for those forthcoming recommendations that will undercut tradition. One alternative is to pass that responsibility to new ad hoc action committees. Another is to make the building of support an integral part of the planning process.

For many volunteer leaders serving on ad hoc committees the submission of a series of carefully and prayerfully thought-out recommendations is the high point of a long and arduous process that required long months of meetings. The satisfaction that comes from a good job well done, however, compensates for that sacrificial investment of time and energy. Six months or a year later the disappointment sets in when it appears all of that work was for nought. It now is obvious that none of the major recommendations will be implemented.

One lesson is, do not expect those volunteers to agree to serve on another long-range planning committee! A second lesson is the planning process should include a strategy for implementation, and that is the theme of the last chapter.

For those interested in an author's strategy, this book is the last in what has turned out to be a six-volume series on church planning. The first, *Effective Church Planning* (1979), discusses the larger context for local church planning including some neglected variables such as large group dynamics, the importance of place, and a range of planning models. The second, *Growing Plans* (1983), focused on church growth strategies for different size congregations. The third, *Looking in the Mirror* (1984), provided a series of conceptual frameworks for a self-appraisal of congregational life and ministry. The fourth, *Getting Things Done* (1986), discusses various concepts and skills for leaders who want to make a difference and see results. From this biased perspective it is my best book and comes closest to any to supplementing this latest volume. The fifth, *Choices for Churches* (1990), supplements this book by exploring in greater detail specific courses of action open to various types of congregations.

Finally, I am indebted to the volunteer leaders, the ministers, and the lay staff members I have worked with in parish consultations during these past three decades. These experiences have been my most valuable sources for insights, ideas, questions, anecdotes, lessons, and conclusions. I came to help you as you struggled to understand what the Lord was calling your congregation to be and to do and how to be faithful to that call. I now look back on those visits and realize I took away far more wisdom than I left behind. I am grateful. Thank you all!

CHAPTER ONE

Where and How Do We Intervene?

"I'VE BEEN HERE FOR SIX WEEKS NOW, AND I BELIEVE I HAVE A pretty good understanding of what's been happening, but I'm not sure about where I should begin," reflected the thirty-seven-year-old newly arrived minister of the 305-member Maple Grove Church. "This congregation peaked in size in the late 1950s when church attendance averaged well over 300 and the Sunday school averaged nearly 250. At that time the staff included the senior minister, a full-time director of Christian education, a part-time youth worker, and a part-time choir director-organist as well as a full-time secretary and a half-time bookkeeper. Now we're down to about 140 at worship and maybe 85 in Sunday school. My guess is the median age of the membership is at least fifteen years higher than it was thirty years ago. I know we've got lots of problems, but I don't know where to begin in trying to solve them. We're down to the secretary and myself plus a new part-time choir director, and we have a volunteer to play the organ. Something has to happen, but where do we begin?"

"I have a different problem," explained the forty-four-year-old recently arrived pastor of Calvin Community Church. "My predecessor was the organizing pastor twenty-eight years ago. When he retired last summer, it was pointed out that the average attendance at worship had increased in twenty-four of those twenty-eight years. He did a remarkable job, no question about it. He left a congregation that was averaging nearly seven hundred at Sunday morning worship, an exceptionally competent and loyal staff, and a large group of outstanding volunteer leaders. In addition, three days after he retired, he and his wife moved to a new home seven hundred miles from here, and he told everyone it would be at least four years before he would even consider an invitation to return. In every respect he has been a model predecessor. My problem is I don't think they need me. One of the associate ministers is an excellent preacher. He filled the pulpit about half the Sundays during my predecessor's last two years here, and he preached every Sunday but two during the vacancy period.

"While he has never told me this directly, my impression is he would like to continue to preach at least half the time. We also have an outstanding minister of pastoral care, and for the past several years he also has been handling more and more of the weddings and funerals. The church really doesn't have any serious problems except attendance, which is down about 15 percent from a year ago."

"That's a natural pattern following the departure of a popular long-tenured minister," observed another member of this group of ministers. They were attending a three-day workshop for recently arrived pastors on the theme of succession.

"Sounds to me like you came to a church that really doesn't have a vacancy for a new senior minister," observed another participant.

★ ★ ★

"We have a good church, and please don't misunderstand me, I'm not complaining," commented Walter Shannon to his Presbyterian neighbor as they drove along the freeway on their daily seventeen-mile journey from home to work, "but our members are growing older, and we're simply not reaching very many of the young families moving out here. I've talked to our pastor about this, and I've expressed our concern to several members on the Board, but nothing seems to happen. In another fifteen years we'll be a dwindling congregation of white-haired and bald old people. What can I do? How can I get people's attention?"

★ ★ ★

"Twice we've voted down proposals to relocate, and today neither one of the sites we considered purchasing is available," reflected a despairing Paul Myer, an architect and a loyal member of the ninety-seven-year-old First Church. "We have zero off-street parking. One entrance to the sanctuary requires a steep climb up a narrow stairway with nineteen steps and the other involves two flights of stairs. Our fellowship hall is too small, and the low ceiling makes it difficult to hear if more than two people are talking at the same time. The parlor is the only decent room we have for an adult class or meeting room, and the nursery is a moldy room in one corner of the basement. I don't see any future for us in this obsolete building on this tiny parcel of land, but it seems like only a few of us are discontented with the status quo."

★ ★ ★

Each of these comments can be summarized under the same broad umbrella. The speaker is discontented with the status quo, but does not know how or where to intervene in the decision-making process. How do you challenge people's attachment to the status quo? That is the central theme of this book.

Three Predictable Patterns

At this point it may be useful to stop and examine three generalizations that also are part of the context for planning in any institution or organization. The first is one that surfaces repeatedly. Barring the existence of a widely perceived crisis, the status quo tends to be tremendously attractive. Most people prefer the comfort of the status quo to the threat of the unknown. Therefore churches, like other organizations, tend to naturally drift in the direction of what is perceived as a reaffirmation of yesterday. One of the most common mistakes made by those seeking to initiate change is to underestimate the attractiveness of the status quo. This is illustrated by the influence of this year's budget on the proposed budget for next year, in the advantage the incumbent has in a campaign for elective office, or in the duration of what in fact are unhappy marriages. Most people still find the status quo preferable to change.

A second predictable pattern is that in any organization only a relatively small proportion of the people are sufficiently well acquainted with the facts to express informed discontent with the status quo. Perhaps two dozen members of the typical four-hundred-member congregation have a thorough understanding of the financial base, of recent membership trends, of the growth or decline in the Sunday school, of the pastoral care of the members, of the outreach ministries, of the youth program, of the adequacy of the meeting place, and of how this congregation fits into the larger church scene in that community. At the other end of that spectrum at least 40 percent are not sufficiently knowledgeable to be able to initiate informed proposals for change. Some readers from middle-sized and large congregations will insist the proportion of well-informed members is closer to 3 percent. Therefore, it is unreasonable to expect immediate, enthusiastic, informed, and active support for a new idea. While facts are friendly, the status quo often is even friendlier.

Third, most leaders have been taught that it is best "to work through the system" and to seek majority approval. While it is possible to make changes from within the system, and sometimes a majority vote is required, that is not always the best road to change. Most major changes that have long-term significance are initiated from either outside the existing organizational structure or by a tiny minority of insiders. Few are initiated by the majority.

These three generalizations constitute part of the context for developing a strategy to create a new future for your church. They also represent part of the context for responding to that initial question, Where and how do I intervene? Before looking at possible points of intervention, however, one additional question must be raised.

"Why do we need to create a special long-range planning committee?" challenged Terry Vander Meer. "Why not have the Board do that? It seems to me that all we'll be doing is creating unnecessary problems in coordination by appointing another special committee. Our Board members are the best informed people in the church, or at least they should be. Why not ask them to prepare a five-year plan for us?"

One of the debates that has been going on for nearly a century in municipal government has been over where to place the responsibility for planning. The traditional point of view has been that planning should be isolated from the corruption of partisan politics and delegated to a commission of unpaid citizen volunteers who would represent the public interest. This was and continues to be the dominant organizational structure in the United States. As more and more municipalities have added professional planners to the payroll, usually they are assigned to staff that commission of unpaid citizen volunteers.

In a book first published just before World War II that eventually became a classic, Robert Walker declared that this was not working. Walker urged, "Planning is one of the staff functions and should be attached to the executive office."[1] In many larger cities the planning director has become a member of the mayor's or city manager's professional staff but that continues to be the exception. Walker's thesis appealed to academicians, to theorists, and to many planners, but not to the general public who feared an excessive accumulation of power in the municipal executive's office.

A logical parallel to Walker's thesis would be to assign the responsibility for planning to the pastor, or perhaps to the governing board of a congregation. This would be consistent with Terry Vander Meer's point stated earlier. Why clutter up the organizational landscape with one more committee?

The first reason is that many pastors are unprepared or unwilling to accept that responsibility. Ministers usually prefer to identify themselves as a preacher or teacher or pastor or friend or counselor or scholar rather than as an administrator. When parish pastors are asked to rank their preferences among their many assignments, administration usually comes in last or next to last.

A second reason is the governing board in most congregations tends to resemble a standing committee. As will be pointed out in greater detail later, by nature standing committees predictably are more comfortable with continuity, stability, a ten-to-eighteen-month time frame, overseeing and maintaining continuing responsibilities, resisting change, and attracting replacement members who are comfortable with the status quo. Rarely do standing committees either initiate or oversee major changes. If a congregation should decide, for example, to construct a new addition, typically the responsibility for that change is assigned to a special ad hoc building planning committee, not to the trustees. Likewise many congregations do not assign the responsibility for calling a new minister to a standing committee on personnel. Instead a special ad hoc committee is created. Only rarely do standing committees accept and fulfill that responsibility for long-range planning.

Part of the reason is in the selection process. Different criteria will be used to select members of a governing board than will be used to pick the people to serve on a long-range planning committee. Perhaps more important, the future should be the only concern of long-range planning committees. By contrast, the agenda at that monthly meeting of the governing board often is dominated by yesterday (minutes, treasurer's report, communications from committees) and today.

Finally, from a pragmatic perspective, it rarely works to expect the governing board to function as a long-range planning committee. The expectations usually exceed the performance.

This discussion provides the context for examining how the status quo can be challenged effectively.

Potential Points of Intervention

Where and how does a person who is interested in change intervene in the ongoing life of the organization that is designed to reinforce and perpetuate the status quo? That is a question that is not unique to the church. It comes up in public education, business, the delivery of health care services, law enforcement, government, publishing, the military services,[2] the airlines, and every other facet of our society.

While less than the most desirable, by far the most wide-open point for potential intervention is a widely recognized crisis. This may take the form of a loss of customers, a fire, a flood, barely winning an election, the unexpected sudden death of the key leader, a financial crisis, or some other disaster. Whenever wide agreement exists on the fact that a crisis does exist, this normally results in a high degree of receptivity for new ideas and sometimes even for an endorsement of radical change. A crisis opens the door to intervention. It should be noted, however, that sometimes people refuse to recognize the existence of a crisis and reject intervention. Thus a more accurate statement is that a widespread *perception* of a crisis is needed.

A second, and a very common point of intervention, may be the annual process to prepare next year's budget. While it is tempting to replicate the current budget, with perhaps a few modest changes, the budget preparation process can be a convenient time to reallocate the priorities in the allocation of resources. If that is to be the critical point of intervention, it may be wise to appoint a special ad hoc study committee to examine priorities and goals several months before the beginning of the process of preparing the budget for the coming year. A variation on that approach is to turn that process into a three-year effort. The budget preparation committee will be asked to bring in specific recommendations on expenditures for the coming year accompanied by budgetary goals for each of the following two years. These should be presented within the context of clearly defined ministry goals for the next three to five years.

A better way to use the budget preparation process as a point of intervention is to ignore last year's budget. Instead of beginning with detailed budget categories, such as insurance, salaries, utilities, postage, printing, and building maintenance, begin with proportions. For example, a common approach in larger congregations is to begin with the expectation that maintenance of the building and debt service will require 15 percent of all expenditures made from current income; staff salaries, and benefits including housing will require 40 percent; 30 percent will be allocated to benevolences and missions; while program and office expenses will need 15 percent. Those proportions can be discussed and refined in the meetings of the budget committee until agreement has been reached on what the proportions should be. That recommendation can be forwarded to the governing board for review and approval. The agreed upon percentages become the framework for the specific allocation of anticipated receipts. This can be a useful means of intervention in those congregations where (a) serious discontent has surfaced as a result of the priorities represented in past budgets and/or (b) expenditures have been exceeding receipts and/or (c) the budget preparation process usually begins with an acceptance of the priorities represented in last year's budget.

Incidentally, in small congregations with a full-time resident pastor those proportions may be closer to 60 percent for staff compensation including all benefits, 15 percent for program and office expenses, 15 percent for benevolences, and 10 percent for debt service and building maintenance.

A third type of intervention may occur when a group of discontented members draws up a petition and secures signatures on that petition. The right by the ruled to petition the rulers is a classic right deeply enshrined in Anglo-Saxon political theory. Too often, however, in the churches it results in the creation of an adversarial relationship. The circulation of petitions that never are formally submitted to the official leadership can inform the grapevine, broaden the base of discontent, and identify potential allies. (This process also may eliminate from that list those who had been perceived as potential allies, but their oral response to a request to sign that petition made it clear they really have a strong attachment to the status quo or they are reluctant to be accused of rocking the boat.)

One of the more highly visible methods of intervention in congregational life is the appearance of the skilled, persuasive, respected, influential, and effective leader who (a) has a vision of a new and different tomorrow, (b) can persuasively communicate that vision to others, and (c) is able and willing to make the effort to win allies who will help translate that vision into reality.

Sometimes that person is a volunteer lay leader. More often that effective initiator of planned change is the pastor. The vast majority of ministers, however, are unwilling or unable to accept that interventionist role. At least a few fail because they do not have a vision of a new and different tomorrow. They, too, are captives of the status quo. Some have a vision but cannot communicate it persuasively so that it becomes a widely shared vision. Others fail to build that supportive coalition necessary to translate that vision into reality. Many more conclude this unilateral approach to initiating change is not compatible with their values, gifts, skills, priorities, personality, and/or with their self-identified leadership role. While male ministers may be more willing to accept this role as an interventionist than is true of today's female pastors, a reasonable estimate is 75 percent of today's pastors are not comfortable and effective with this approach to planned change. As a group, senior pastors of larger churches are more likely to accept this interventionist role than are ministers serving middle-sized and smaller congregations.

Some will argue that this leadership role, which calls for the pastor to be the initiator of planned change, is (a) incompatible with the dream of the ministry of the laity, (b) inconsistent with what is taught in most theological seminaries, (c) inappropriate in the majority of congregations averaging fewer than a hundred at worship, (d) incompatible with the polity or system of congregational governance in those denominations that grant considerable authority to volunteer leaders, and (e) incompatible with the personality profiles of the majority of the graduates of theological seminaries.

Despite all these reservations, the most effective means of challenging the status quo is for the newly arrived minister who is a skilled agent of intentional change initiated from within an organization, who displays an attractive personality, who is a highly productive worker, who is able and willing to earn the trust of the people, and who has a vision of a new and better tomorrow to accept that leadership role!

What Are the Choices?

If, however, it is unrealistic to expect the governing board of the congregation or any of the standing committees or a volunteer leader or the pastor to be an effective proponent of planned change initiated from within that parish, what are the alternatives?

One, as explained earlier, is to wait for the arrival of the widely perceived crisis.

A second, as mentioned earlier, is to ask the committee preparing next year's budget to accept the role of interventionist. This usually fails. One reason is the power of yesterday in preparing budgets. A second is that a crisis in budget preparation usually fosters creativity for cutting back, not for expanding ministry. A third is represented by that ancient budget officer's admonition, "It is extremely difficult to introduce anything new into next year's budget. It is even more difficult to delete anything that has been in the budget for three or more years."

A third alternative is to secure the services of an outside third party who has the skills and personality required to be an effective interventionist. This parish consultant may come from the staff of a regional or national denominational agency or it may be the pastor of a similar congregation or it may be a professional parish consultant.

A fourth alternative is to create an ad hoc special futures committee or long-range planning committee. That is the subject of this book. That also may be the most attractive alternative for the majority of Protestant congregations on the North American continent.

Why?

Another perspective that may be useful in defending the creation of a special ad hoc committee can be found in a more detailed examination of a few of the essential differences among three types of committees.

1. Standing committees tend to (a) see themselves as charged with the continuity, oversight, and maintenance of

their assigned responsibilities, (b) feel free to mobilize resources including volunteers and perhaps even to seek designated second-mile financial contributions, although many standing committees have to exist within the limits of budgeted expenditures, (c) function within a relatively short time frame for planning—especially in those organizations that require rotation in office and limit tenure to three years—this means the majority of that committee, often including the chairperson, have fewer than twenty-four months left before being rotated off that committee, (d) naturally resist change since their basic responsibility is continuity, (e) attract people who are comfortable with continuity and are not excited by proposals for change—frequently when a specific assignment is being discussed the first question is, What did we do last year?—and (f) be reluctant to expand their jurisdiction or invade the turf of other committees—when this is suggested, a common response is, "But that's not one of our responsibilities, that's the job of the thus-and-so committee."

In summary, standing committees usually do not color outside the lines, and they assume everything is prohibited unless specifically permitted.

2. The ad hoc study committee is a completely different breed of institutional creature.

At least nine expectations can be identified about the actions of the typical study committee. First, it can be expected to challenge the status quo. If everyone was completely satisfied with how things are going, there would not be a need for a study committee. Second, the study committee can be expected to recommend changes, including some that will be seen as unnecessarily disruptive by members of standing committees. Third, study committees can be expected to attract as members people who are of a reflective nature, who are comfortable conceptualizing abstract ideas, and who are less than completely satisfied with the status quo. Fourth, study committees can and usually should be expected to plan within a time frame of at least two to five years and perhaps as long as two or three decades. Fifth, study committees can be expected to bring in two or more alternatives as they recommend changing the status quo, but often fail to do so unless specifically instructed.

Sixth, in an effort to reach a consensus, or sometimes even to be able to produce a majority report, study committees often bring in compromises that represent an effort to bring together two or more substantially different points of view. The greater the emphasis on choosing members of a study committee—so that every group, organization, class, faction, point of view, and value system in the congregation is directly represented on that committee—the more likely that the final recommendation will be the product of compromises. Sometimes the compromises are so great that the final recommendation not only is unacceptable to a majority of the members of the congregation, it also is unacceptable to several influential members of the study committee.

It is not uncommon for this emphasis on diversity in the membership of the committee to result in a high degree of polarization within the committee. This can be so pronounced that it results in a majority report accompanied by a dissenting minority report. That polarization within the committee can be transferred to polarize the entire congregation via that minority report. A common response to that situation is to appoint a new, and more homogeneous, study committee.

Seventh, only in the smaller congregations is it realistic to expect a study committee to mobilize resources. The study committee comes in with a recommendation for a new program or a new building or the addition of a new staff person or a change in the schedule. Someone else is expected to produce the resources needed to implement that recommendation. The basic rule is study committees study and report, they rarely implement their own recommendation.

Eighth, the more thorough the research and the longer the amount of time devoted to analyzing the problem and the more in-depth the investigation of the situation the committee has been asked to study, the more likely the members will find themselves "out of touch" with the rest of the members. The reason for that is simple. Education is alienating. Most parents of teenagers discover that when their eighteen-year-old returns home at Thanksgiving after being away at college for three months. That fact of life has also been discovered by many empty-nest couples when the forty-six-year-old wife returns to school to get her degree. Special study committees are not exempt from that phenomenon. A simple and common example is the special committee that has been asked to study the staff needs of the larger congregation. It is assumed the study committee will recommend the creation of a new position, but the final recommendation may be to terminate the employment of one or more of the current staff. This recommendation for radical change usually is viewed as unreasonable or demonic by the friends of those staff members who are to be dismissed. The best antidote for this normal and predictable phenomenon is continuing two-way communication between the study committee and the church members.

Finally, the special study committee probably should not be expected to *do* anything. Its job is to study and to recommend, not to do. It is not uncommon for several members of the study committee to be eager to serve on the new committee that is about to be appointed to implement the recommendation of the study committee, but it is unrealistic, except in small congregations, to expect all the members to want to be part of that experience. Some will feel, "I've done my job. It's someone else's turn now."

Frequently, but not always, a long-range planning committee or a futures committee resembles an ad hoc study committee.

3. A third and relatively common type of committee consists of that select group of people who are asked to implement a special course of action. Examples include the building committee responsible for the construction of a new structure, the special committee charged to plan and carry out the celebration of the one hundredth anniversary of the founding of this parish, the group who design and staff the first religious drama to be presented by this congregation to a community-wide audience, the volunteers who plan and implement that highly visible protest challenging a recent decision of the city council or who design and staff the reception to welcome the new pastor, and the task force responsible for organizing the new weekday nursery school.

They, too, display several common characteristics. First, unlike the typical study committees, these ad hoc action committees can be expected to implement a new idea. Second, normally they can be expected to mobilize resources. Third, unlike the typical standing committee, they rarely veto a change in the status quo. They were created to make changes and so change, not continuity, is their guiding light.

Fourth, while most standing committees and some study committees are very careful about overstepping their limits, the action committee rarely feels that constraint. Standing committees often act on the assumption that everything is prohibited except that which is permitted. Special action committees are more likely to act on the assumption that everything is permitted unless it is specifically prohibited. They rarely feel guilty about coloring outside the lines.

Fifth, special action committees tend to attract the activists, those who are optimistic about the future, those who enjoy doing more than reflecting, and those who are discontented with the status quo. They attract people who are open to change.

Finally, frequently special action committees have the most fun. They usually are asked to create something new rather than to maintain the status quo. They also enjoy the satisfaction of a terminal date. Frequently, but not always, persons who have enjoyed their service on two or three action committees become bored with the routine of serving on the typical standing committee. In larger congregations it is not uncommon to find several long-time and dedicated members who refuse all requests to serve on standing committees. They are receptive only to invitations to join a new action committee. Once they have seen Paris, it is hard to keep them down on the farm.

Summary

If these reflections about the characteristics of these three different types of committees match your experience, you can see why these differences should be recognized in projecting expectations on committees. What are reasonable expectations?

First, in a typical year most congregations will benefit from the work of several standing committees, at least one special action committee, and perhaps a study committee. Each one has a distinctive contribution to make, and that should be recognized and celebrated.

Second, and most important, a recognition of the differences among these committees can help minimize placing unrealistic expectations on any one committee. Do not expect what is not realistic to expect.

Third, instead of selecting committee members on the basis of quotas or to make sure every group and faction is directly represented, it may be more productive to select people on the basis of their gifts, talents, skills, and experiences. Match the gifts to the appropriate committee. This is especially important in selecting members of a special action committee or a long-range planning committee.

Fourth, when someone proposes a new idea, decide how it should be handled. If you want it rejected, refer it to a standing committee. If you decide it needs refining and improving, send it to a special study committee. If it has obvious merit and deserves to be implemented, create a special ad hoc committee and direct its members to turn that new proposal into reality.

Fifth, only in rare circumstances should the work of a special action committee be financed out of the regular church budget. This type of committee normally has the capability to mobilize resources. Therefore, rather than place it in a competitive situation with the standing committees in the allocation of scarce resources in the regular budget preparation process, encourage the special action committee to raise its own money and enlist its own volunteer workers.

Sixth, as will be emphasized repeatedly throughout this book, do not expect a standing committee also to function as a long-range planning committee! Only rarely are standing committees comfortable functioning in the three-to-five-year time frame that is necessary for long-range planning.

Seventh, scale your expectations to the size and expectations of the congregations. The congregation averaging fewer than one hundred at Sunday morning worship may need only three or four standing committees plus an occasional special action committee. The congregation that averages between one hundred and two hundred at worship may need a half dozen or more standing committees plus a couple of ad hoc action committees every year.

The numerically growing congregation that is experiencing considerable discontinuity often will find it helpful for the ad hoc study committees and action task forces to outnumber the standing committees.

By the time the average attendance at worship passes one thousand, the standing committees, with their emphasis on continuity, their natural desire to try to keep everything simple, and their reluctance to endorse change may become a significant barrier to expanding the ministry of that congregation. One response is to not expand. Another is to transfer more authority to the staff, to ad hoc study committees, and to special action committees.

As the congregation continues to grow in size, the normal tendency is to place greater responsibility on the staff for both the oversight of programs and for the administration of the parish. A large proportion of the superchurches that average more than three thousand at Sunday morning worship do not utilize any standing committees. All the responsibilities for administrative and programmatic decisions are placed on the staff or given to ad hoc action committees. The Board focuses its effort on direction and on preparing for tomorrow. With that one exception of the Board, all the emphasis on the role of the laity is to enlist, train, and support them as volunteers in ministry, both within the congregation and to the world. A variety of training events are offered to enhance the competence of the members as counselors, teachers, preachers, shepherds, and missionaries or to prepare them for special ministries such as with people in prison, or with those who are recovering from divorce, or to teach classes of newlyweds, or to work with youth. No effort, however, is devoted to training people to serve as policy makers on standing committees.

It may not be irrelevant to note that those denominations that require an elaborate system of administrative and programmatic standing committees rarely include congregations that average more than three thousand at Sunday morning worship.

Finally, honor the preferences of those who prefer to serve

on a particular type of committee. Do not force someone who prefers to serve on a standing committee to be a member of a special action committee. Do not ask outfielders to play short-stop. Do not pressure those who enjoy working on a special ad hoc committee to serve on a standing committee.

People can enjoy serving on committees if their gifts and skills are matched with the appropriate type of committee—and that raises the issue of the criteria to be used in selecting members of your long-range planning committee if you decide to choose that as the method of intervention for challenging the status quo.

CHAPTER TWO

Creating That Committee

"BEFORE WE GET TOO FAR INTO MAKING ANY SPECIFIC RECOM-mendations, I think we ought to find out how our people really feel about how things are going here," urged Stanley Henderson. "Why don't we schedule a series of cottage meetings and invite our members to come to one of them and give us a chance to hear their hopes and dreams for this church? We have about four hundred members, and if we scheduled twenty of these listening meetings, that would mean an average of twenty people per meeting."

"I don't need to go to twenty more meetings," protested Jack Kramer.

"Oh, that wouldn't be necessary," explained Stanley. "With twelve of us on this futures committee, we could divide that up among us. If two of us went to each cottage meeting, that would be only three or four meetings for each one of us. I really do believe we need to listen to what our people have to say. That should be an essential ingredient in our planning process."

"I would be amazed if we got as many as a hundred and fifty of our members to come to one of these cottage meetings," declared Dorothy Weston. "I'm not opposed to your idea, Stanley, but when we have fewer than two hundred of our members at worship on the typical Sunday morning, I doubt if we'll get four hundred to come to cottage meetings."

"That's okay," agreed Stanley cheerfully. "The important thing is the process, and that means we give everyone a chance to be heard."

"Heard on what?" questioned Laura Phillips. "What will they respond to at these cottage meetings? This is the first meeting of this futures committee. What can we offer for an agenda for these meetings?"

Rather than begin their process with a divisive quarrel, the majority of the membership of that futures committee gave in to Stanley Henderson and his two allies. Twenty cottage meetings were scheduled at twenty different homes. The congregation was given a list of the dates and places and the members were invited to pick the one that fit their schedule or was close to where they lived. The theme was, "We want to hear your hopes and dreams for our church."

This process used up the first fifteen weeks of the futures committee's schedule. Twenty meetings were scheduled. One was cancelled by the host family because of the illness of the husband, and the three people who did appear (two of whom were members of the committee) were instructed to pick another time and place. Twenty-nine members attended the one held at the home of the most widely respected leader of that congregation, and twenty-one attended the one hosted by the pastor. The other seventeen reported a combined total attendance of 114 including children. Thirty-two of those 114 were representatives from the futures committee. The total process involved all twelve members of the futures committee, 99 other members, plus 29 children. Nearly three-quarters of the confirmed membership stayed away from all of these cottage meetings. The one held at the pastor's home was the most constructive. The fifty-three-year-old pastor, who had attended two other unstructured cottage meetings earlier that were largely gripe sessions, prepared for this one and developed a list of a dozen open-ended questions that were used to guide the discussion. That list included these questions:

What do you believe the Lord is calling this church to be and to do today and tomorrow?

What do you want this church to look like five years from today?

What do you believe we do best in ministry today?

What do you believe should be our number-one point of excellence five years from now?

What changes should be made in our real estate?

How do you believe non-members view our church today?

How do you want non-members to perceive this congregation five years from now?

The answers to these and other questions could be summarized in one sentence. What we want for tomorrow is a church that is much like today only better, more faithful, more loving, more caring, and more committed.

Most of the responses from these nineteen cottage meetings could be placed in one of four categories.

1. The most numerous were more of the same, only better.

2. The second most numerous were irrelevant gripes and complaints.

3. The third most numerous were relevant gripes and complaints about a huge variety of concerns ranging from how loud the organ should be played to the lack of commitment in many members to the poor acoustics for the pews under the balcony to the absence of anyone in the office on Saturdays to a desire for a greater emphasis on the Holy Scriptures to the contents of the new hymnal to more frequent services that included Holy Communion to the lack of clarity on the purpose of these cottage meetings.

4. The least frequent responses were constructive suggestions. These included specific proposals to expand the staff, to reduce total expenditures, to increase the proportion of total expenditures allocated to missions, to remodel the present building, to relocate and construct a new meetinghouse on a larger site four miles away, to restructure the Sunday school, to expand the Sunday morning schedule, to adopt a more aggressive stance on issue-centered ministries, to add a Saturday evening worship service, to increase the number of adult Bible study classes, to instruct the pastor to devote more time to calling on shut-ins, to purge the membership roster to a more realistic total, to improve the quality of the youth program, and to attract more younger families.

What happened here?

Everything that happened can be described as normal, natural, and predictable institutional behavior. The entire sequence is vulnerable to only four criticisms. One mistake was scheduling these cottage meetings *before* the futures committee had specific proposals to recommend to the members. This could have been a constructive experience if the futures committee had reached the point in their deliberations where they could have reported, "We are convinced our church is at a fork in the road. We believe this church has two choices open to it. One is Proposal A. The other is Proposal B. One will take us in one direction. The other will take us in a substantially different direction. We are mailing copies of these two proposals to every household. Next month we will hold a series of cottage meetings at which both proposals will be explained in more detail. Everyone will have an opportunity to attend the meeting of your choice, to raise your questions, and to offer comments, criticisms, and suggestions. We have reached the stage in our deliberations where we need your responses. Please read the report carefully and plan to attend one of these cottage meetings."

In other words, one mistake was to schedule these cottage meetings prematurely. As was pointed out in chapter 1, when people are asked to respond to a choice between the status quo and a vague, open-ended and unarticulated dream about the future, most will express a preference for an improved version of today. They may not agree, however, on the details of that improved version of the status quo.

Participation or Performance?

Perhaps the clearest way to make this point is to distinguish between participation and performance. Normally a special long-range planning committee will not be created unless discontent with the status quo exists. This usually means the primary focus is on the performance of that congregation. This discontent may be caused by a dwindling Sunday school, a financial crisis, the inadequacy of the physical facilities, an inability to reach younger generations, a decline in worship attendance, problems with the schedule, the need for more staff, or some other concerns.

This creates expectations for recommendations for improving performance. That special ad hoc committee is expected to make an accurate diagnosis of the situation and suggest a positive course of action. As a general rule, the larger the number of members, the greater the proportion who are concerned with quality and performance. The smaller the size of the congregation, the broader the concern that "my voice be heard in policy making." In larger churches the vast majority of the people want results, not participation.

The other side of this issue is the distinction between voice and vote. In most Protestant congregations on the North American continent the majority of members are more than willing to grant full authority to a futures committee to prepare a recommended course of action. They really are not interested in having a voice in that process. Depending on the polity, however, most will want to have a vote on the implementation of that recommended course of action. The two most common means of casting that vote are with their (a) presence or absence and (b) financial support. The high level of performance usually wins strong votes of affirmation. The low level of performance results in absent people and absent dollars. As will be discussed in more detail in chapter 5, this usually means the futures committee should be more concerned with performance and quality than with listening to an endless stream of complaints, gripes, uninformed diagnostic statements, mutually incompatible recommendations, and premature evaluations.

Informed or Uninformed Discussions?

A second error was made by the majority of the members of this futures committee when they yielded to Stanley Henderson's proposal to schedule this series of cottage meetings. Laura Phillips had raised an important issue when she asked about an agenda for these meetings. The critical debate is not over that process for securing opinions and responses from the members. Laura had raised a key point. Do we want an informed discussion or an uninformed discussion? The majority yielded to Stanley Henderson's proposal to schedule an uninformed process. That was the second mistake.

One of the prices the committee subsequently paid for that mistake was in responding to those four sets of responses evoked by this uninformed process.

Who Should Not Be on It?

The third, and perhaps the most obvious, mistake was made by the person(s) who selected Stanley Henderson to be a member of this futures committee. The only persuasive defense that can be offered for that choice was that a quota system was required by that congregation's constitution for the selection of leaders and Stanley was chosen to represent (a) those who believe strongly in counterproductive decision-making practices and/or (b) those who are unable or unwilling to examine potential consequences before making a decision with long-term implications.

To be more precise, Stanley Henderson represents one of five categories of people who should *not* be asked to serve on your long-range planning committee.

A second is represented by Jackie Brown. At the first meeting of the long-range planning committee, Jackie is likely to make statements such as these.

1. "I know that a lot of people complain about the lack of parking here, but that is not a problem. I come to the eight-thirty service on Sunday morning, and I've never had a problem finding a place to park within a block or two of the front door. I don't believe we have a parking problem."

This ignores (a) the peak hour problem, (b) the plight of first-time visitors who arrive at ten-fifty-eight for the eleven o'clock service because of difficulty in finding this address and have to search for four or five minutes to find a parking space, (c) the shortage of parking for weekday programming when the two-hour restrictions apply for all nearby street parking, (d) the difficulties encountered by those who come to an evening meeting when it is raining, (e) the shortage of convenient parking for any very large group event, and (f) the importance of convenient parking if this church is to reach new generations of people.

2. "When I was a teenager, this is how they ran the youth program in the church I was in back in 1958, and I think that's the way we should do it here today."

This statement overlooks the fact that few of today's teenagers are replicas of the people who were teenagers back in 1958.[1]

3. "There has to be a limit to how far we can go in accommodating people! The more you give in to what people say they want, the more they demand. I think it is time we take a stand and say, 'That's it!' We need to draw a line somewhere and I believe the time has come to draw it."

A third person who should not be asked to serve on the long-range planning committee is represented by Hank Lansford. Hank's prime complaint is that this congregation already is too large, too impersonal, too complex, too liberal (or conservative), and making too many changes too fast.

Instead of inviting Hank to be on the long-range planning committee, it might be more productive to encourage him to find a church home where he would be happy. The three objections to that alternative are (1) that it represents an unforgiving stance, (2) that it could arouse a severe internal disruption created by Hank's relatives, and/or (3) that such a church may not exist.

A fourth person who should not be asked to serve on the long-range planning committee is the pastor's number-one opponent or enemy or one who leads the movement seeking the pastor's resignation or early retirement. That voice on the futures committee often will lead to diversionary discussions about how "all of our problems would be solved by finding a new minister."

Finally, the fifth person who should not be asked to serve on the long-range planning committee is the individual who insists on recreating 1914 and making this into a geographical parish designed to serve those people who live within walking distance of the church property.

The three big objections to this dream are (a) the automobile may be here to stay, (b) most of the people who choose a church on the basis of geographical proximity were born before 1930 while the future of most churches is with the people born after 1930, and (c) most of the people who live within walking distance of your church do not want to come to your church—and rarely can you force them to come.

Avoid Self-Defeating Behavior!

The fourth and perhaps the most serious error made by that futures committee occurred when no one in that group identified and challenged the bias built into the process proposed by Stanley Henderson. While Stanley undoubtedly believed this was a neutral, democratic, and creative process, it is not without bias. Partly because it is an uninformed process, as was pointed out earlier, and partly because of the nature of that open-ended process, it is biased against change and in favor of the status quo.

The results of that series of cottage meetings described earlier illustrate that point. When people are given a choice between maintaining the status quo and change, the natural tendency is to choose the status quo.

What is wrong with that? Why not reinforce the status quo?

Rarely is a long-range planning committee created unless people are dissatisfied with contemporary reality. Such a committee usually is appointed as the result of an urge to improve, to change, to create a better tomorrow. If that is the goal, why follow a process designed to reinforce the status quo?

Who Do You Want?

If it is unwise or counterproductive to ask people like Stanley Henderson or Jackie Brown or Hank Lansford to serve on the long-range planning committee, who should be asked? What are the characteristics of the people who will help make this an effective process?

That question can best be answered by first asking, What do

you want to happen? If all that is sought by those leaders who suggested the need for a futures committee is modest improvements on what is now happening, it may be wise to ask that array of standing committees to study how they might improve the quality of their current performance. If, however, at least a few of today's leaders want more than modest qualitative changes, it probably will be necessary to pay the price of discontinuity. That usually means adding new ingredients to today's package of resources and ministry and/or scrapping the old and replacing it with the new.

In other words, if substantial changes are envisioned, it may be useful to follow these criteria in selecting the members of that long-range planning committee. Ideally all, or nearly all, the members will share a common understanding of (1) the New Testament definition of the nature of a worshiping community, (2) what the Lord is calling this congregation to be and to be about today and tomorrow, (3) what this congregation is today including both strengths and limitations, (4) the political realities of this parish including the identification of potential veto groups and the reality of tradeoffs, and (5) the value of open deliberations and of a redundant system for keeping the membership informed about the direction this committee is headed. (See chapter 10 for a more extended discussion on this last point.)

In addition, it helps if all the members (1) are actively supportive of the current pastor, (2) are able and willing to initiate and lead—in other words, include venturesome risk-takers, (3) project a strong future orientation and display little interest in seeking to recreate yesterday—one way of encouraging this is to maximize the number of persons who joined this congregation within the past five years, (4) are comfortable discussing abstract concepts such as purpose, role, and mission, (5) are convinced that potentially the best days of this congregation's history lie in the future, and (6) are active as volunteers in the life and ministry of that congregation. In many long-established congregations it may be prudent to include one or two people who have a positive tie with the grapevine linking together that network of older long-tenured members.

Why Not a Representative Committee?

Many of today's leaders have been taught that broad-based participation in planning and decision-making is an essential ingredient in creating democratic institutions. Therefore, why insist on a homogeneous membership for that futures committee rather than on a more representative group? Why not seek to have every group, organization, class, committee, faction, choir, fellowship, and board represented on this committee?

Perhaps the most obvious reason is that few congregations were designed to function as pure democracies. The vast majority of Christian congregations are organized on the principle of leaders and followers.[2] In most traditions, this is reinforced by a reliance on a paid full-time professionally trained leader called the minister and volunteer followers.

Second, and perhaps most important of all, the initial reason for creating a long-range planning committee usually is because of substantial discontent with contemporary reality. The saddest commentary on participatory democracy and change was offered by Clark Kerr when he pointed out that the only way to assure everyone a sense of meaningful participation and power is to grant everyone a right of veto. Since the only thing that cannot be vetoed is the status quo, participatory democracy has turned out to be a surprisingly effective means of perpetuating the status quo.[3]

Occasionally this demand for broad-based participation by all the members in the planning process is offered under the umbrella of "empowering the laity" or "broadening the base of participation." Perhaps the most unpleasant sentence in this book is aroused by that cry. The record reveals that the greater the emphasis on participatory democracy in planning and policy formulation, the more likely that organization will repel the people it is seeking to reach.[4]

Thus if change is the goal, it may not be realistic to expect a representative committee to produce recommendations for change. Every history of organizations, institutions, and nations reveals that major changes are initiated by a tiny minority, not a majority. The only exception, as was pointed out earlier, is when a widespread perception of a crisis exists.

A third reason for following the route of homogeneity is size. The goal of representing every group, organization, class, committee, faction, age, cohort, choir, fellowship, and board usually means creating a committee of fifteen to thirty-five members. If change is the goal, the ideal size of the long-range planning committee is five to seven with nine as an absolute maximum. A seven-member committee can enjoy most of the benefits of small group dynamics, include a broad range of personalities and ages, function as a source of mutually inspired creativity, minimize internal conflict, bring forth a report with unanimous support and without serious compromises, and conclude the whole process in a reasonable period of time.

A fourth generalization that is relevant here is that the larger the number of members on that futures committee, the greater the probability that collection of people will focus on problems, rather than on potentialities, will be diverted by means-to-an-end concerns, will be unable to agree on direction, goals, and priorities, and will be forced to accept least-common-denominator compromises in order to secure majority support for the final report. The model should be the lovers' discussions on setting the date for the wedding, not the writing of the party platform at a political convention.

Finally, the smaller the size of the committee, the more likely the pastor or the senior minister can be an influential part of the process without dominating it. When asked to work with a futures committee that is a representation of the entire membership and includes two or three dozen members, the pastor is tempted to choose one of two alternatives. The easier is to drift over to the sidelines and mentally criticize the pace, direction, and content of the discussion. A second is to move in and become the convenor-chairperson-agenda-setter-leader-teacher-secretary and dominant personality who ends up writing that critical first draft of the final report.

If the goal is a more collegial leadership role for the pastor that includes creating an informed coalition that will be active and persuasive supporters of the final recommendation, a committee of five to seven including the minister should be seen as the ideal size. That means it will be too small—except in the nineteen-member congregation—to be a representative cross section of the membership.

The last comment on size is to compare the twenty household congregation with the one that includes six hundred households. In the former a powerful argument for the fifteen-member committee is that most of the families and every leader can be included in those deliberations. A thirty-member committee in the six-hundred-household church usually means 95 or 96 percent of all households will *not* be directly represented. Changing to a seven-member committee offers many advantages and means 99 percent of all households will *not* be directly represented. Are the disadvantages that go with that big committee worth that small increase in representation? Probably not.

Who Chooses Them?

For some people the most sensitive issue in creating a long-range planning committee is not size or homogeneity or process, but rather who will choose the members. No one answer will fit all situations, but three variables can be of help.

The first, and perhaps the most obvious, is to ask to whom the committee will report. The congregation? The governing board? The executive committee of the governing board? A standing committee? The pastor? The regional judicatory of that denomination? Who is the client?

An argument can be made that the number-one client either should choose the membership of the long-range planning committee or at least confirm the nominees.

In some churches a constitutionally mandated nominating committee nominates the membership of all committees, and that includes both ad hoc and standing committees. In other traditions the governing board chooses the members of ad hoc committees. In real life the larger the number of members of that congregation, the greater the probability the pastor will exercise considerable influence in the selection process.

A second variable is the leadership role of the pastor. If the pastor chooses a reactive, rather than an initiating role, it is not uncommon for the pastor to allow or encourage someone else to name members of the long-range planning committee. Some of these pastors refuse to accept a voting membership on such a committee and at least a few only rarely attend the committee's meetings. That may be an appropriate role for the minister of the very small congregation that changes pastors every two or three years or for the smallest congregation in a yoked arrangement that calls for one minister to serve three or four or five or six congregations or for the pastor who plans to depart within the next three months.

At the other end of that spectrum are the pastors who choose a more aggressive leadership role and who often initiate the idea of creating a long-range planning committee. These pastors usually expect to play an influential role in the deliberations of that committee and that influential role begins with the selection of the members. (If that strong leader is in the final months of that pastorate and will soon be moving, it probably would be wise either to postpone formation of this committee until after the arrival of the successor or to ask the nominating committee to select the membership.)

The Greatest Danger

Perhaps the greatest risk in creating a long-range planning committee is that one of these five alternatives will constitute the eventual outcome. The first is a careless selection process that nominates people who hold irreconcilable views for this committee. Sometimes it is hoped that by serving together these members will reach a common understanding. That is asking for at least a middle-sized miracle. The more likely result is a watered-down recommendation or the complete inability of the committee to agree on a course of action. This can be a waste of valuable time.

The second danger is when the departing minister insists on creating the committee and leaves shortly after it has been selected. The new minister may disown the entire process and the committee members feel completely isolated from the new pastor. The reason they feel that way is because they are isolated from that new pastor.

A third risk is that the committee may operate in isolation from the ongoing life of the congregation, and a receptive audience does not exist when the committee's report is presented. (See chapter 10.)

Fourth, it is not uncommon for one or two volunteer leaders to be the most creative, enthusiastic, future-oriented, optimistic, and daring members of that committee. If one or both leave two-thirds of the way through the committee's deliberations, that can undermine the whole venture. That is one more reason why the selection process is so critical. That whole effort should not be designed to be dependent on one or two volunteers!

Finally, it is possible that the whole effort may be oversold. The rest of the members of that congregation may persuade themselves that the creation of a long-range planning committee is the painless way to solve all problems. This committee is expected to bring forth a painless or magical set of recommendations that will make everyone happy, require no tradeoffs, and will produce a new and better tomorrow without disruptive changes.

One answer to that dream is there is no gain without pain. Another is to encourage reasonable expectations, but that is another chapter.

CHAPTER THREE

What Are Reasonable Expectations?

"AS PART OF MY PREPARATION FOR SERVING ON THIS COMMITTEE, I invited Jim and Betty Haines over for dinner last week," explained Esther Brown, a sixty-two-year-old widow and an active leader in Central Church. "Some of you may know Jim Haines. He is now completing his ninth year as the senior minister over at the First Presbyterian Church. When my husband and I moved here thirty-nine years ago, First Pres was the biggest and strongest church in town. At least half of the movers and shakers in this community were members over there. When their minister, who was reported to be the best preacher in this state, retired, the congregation fell on hard times. During the next twenty-five years a lot of their core members retired, died, or left to join other churches. When Jim Haines came nine years ago, their attendance was less than a fourth of what it had been back at the peak. Jim told me that on his first Sunday, all he saw was bald and grey heads scattered among a sea of empty pews."

"That's not what it is today," interrupted attorney Jeff Davis, one of the seven members of the long-range planning committee at Central Church who were gathered for their first meeting. "Two of my law partners are members of First Pres, and they're always bragging about the great youth program, the big classes of young couples in the Sunday school, the superb music, and the huge amounts of money they give to missions. We just moved here five years ago, and that was considered to be one of the best churches in town when we came. My wife and I visited there twice while we were church shopping, but we decided we didn't want to switch denominations, so we finally decided to come here to Central. How did they reverse their decline? Maybe we can adopt their secret of success to our situation here at Central."

"That's why I wanted to talk with Jim and Betty," continued Esther. "I wanted to find out firsthand what had happened over there and how they had pulled it off. Jim told me that he spent the first six or eight weeks sizing up the situation, and then he developed what he calls his 'Great Design.'[1] This was a nine-step plan that began with replacing the seventy-three-year-old choir director. He had been at First Pres for over forty years and, according to Jim, was clearly over the hill."

"That's true," affirmed Laura Williams. "He lived down the street from us, and my husband's parents knew him real well. I remember when they stopped by our house late one evening after the farewell dinner for that choir director. They said it was really a sad event because everyone there felt he should have retired at least three or four years earlier."

"Jim said his first step was to replace that choir director with a minister of music who was called to build a big music program," continued Esther as she pulled her notes out of her purse. "Today they have fourteen different music groups, and the music staff includes a full-time minister of music plus six part-time people, and nearly three hundred volunteers are involved one way or another in that ministry. To make a long story short, Jim told me the next eight steps of his Grand Design were to expand the adult Sunday school, hire a full-time person to create an attractive youth program, revitalize the women's fellowship, organize a men's Saturday morning prayer breakfast, persuade the Session to adopt a policy that the first twenty-five cents of every dollar would be allocated to missions, arrange to purchase adjacent property and clear it for more off-street parking, completely renovate their seventy-year-old educational building and air-condition the sanctuary, and finally to organize a Monday-through-Saturday Early Childhood Development Center which includes a nursery school for three- and four-year-olds Monday through Friday plus a Saturday morning Youth Club program."

"That's quite a story," declared Agnes Woods. "How in the

world did a church that had been declining for twenty-five years attract that kind of minister?"

"That's an interesting story in itself," replied Esther. "Jim told me that when he and his wife were divorced sixteen years ago, he resigned from the church he had been serving and took a call to a much smaller congregation in Pennsylvania. That's where he met Betty. She had been widowed eight years earlier and was teaching kindergarten. Jim was forty-eight and Betty was thirty-six when they were married. Four years later a friend told Jim he should put his name in the hat for First Presbyterian Church. They had been searching for a new pastor for nearly two years and every attractive candidate they interviewed turned them down because this obviously was a dying downtown church without any future. Jim said he really didn't expect to even be asked to come for an interview since he was over fifty and also had been divorced. According to Betty, Jim was head and shoulders above any of the other candidates they were considering, so they called him despite his age and divorce. Now, of course, they're delighted with what has happened since he came. Betty was the one who organized their special ministry with younger widows several years ago. She was only twenty-eight when her husband was killed. She also was the key person in creating their Early Childhood Development Center. As you may know, they have two adopted children; one is fourteen and the other is now seventeen."

"I grew up in the Presbyterian Church," said Jamie McLeod. "What was the role of the Session in all of this? The only time you've mentioned them was when the minister asked them to approve a policy on how much money would be allocated to missions. In a Presbyterian congregation the Session usually is a powerful group, and I expect in an old downtown church the Session would include some very influential individuals."

"That's exactly what Jim told me," replied Esther. "I don't know whether this was part of his Grand Design or not, but he explained that by the time he came as the fifty-two-year-old new minister, he had been around the block a few times himself. He explained he had a four-part strategy in working with that governing board. First, he says he believes in what he described as incremental change. That means a one-at-a-time approach to introducing new ideas to the Session. Second, he said he always enlisted three or four of his elders as active allies for every new idea or program before he ever brought it up before the whole governing board. Third, he said, as far as practical, he tried to bring new members on the Session who were younger than himself and who had joined since he came. Finally, he always insisted that a minimum of three months go by between the time he introduced a new idea and when the Session voted on it. That gave the recalcitrant elders time to talk themselves into supporting it or to be persuaded by other elders. Now, of course, he has the unqualified support of the Session and the only big disagreement is that Jim wants to retire in three or four years when he will be sixty-five and the Session wants him to keep on at least six or seven more years."

"This has been an instructive lesson, and I want to thank you, Esther, for your provocative report," declared Alfredo Javier, who had been elected to chair this newly created committee. "Maybe we should prepare a grand design for Central Church."

★ ★ ★

"You know, we may be creating a lot of trouble for ourselves," reflected David Watson, a thirty-nine-year-old accountant and a member of the futures committee of the Western Hills Community Church. This congregation had been organized in 1957 and met in a building on a one-acre site directly across the street from what originally had been an elementary school in the middle of a residential subdivision that first opened in 1953. What once had been a community of young families was now populated largely by mature couples and widows, plus a growing number of single parent mothers who had moved back to live with their parents. Nearly all of what once had been described as "tract houses" had been remodeled at least twice and today no two looked exactly alike. The variety of mature trees also reduced the sense of homogeneity. The elementary school was now a community center operated by the local park district.

"We were instructed to come back with a recommendation between renovating this thirty-three-year-old building or razing the two houses we own next to our original one-acre site and constructing a big general purpose room plus a couple of classrooms," continued David. "This is our seventh meeting, and if I understand the sense of this group correctly, one of us favors remodeling the original building, two support the new construction proposal, and six of us are convinced we don't have a very bright future at this location. I grew up in this church and my parents still live within an eighth of a mile of where we're meeting tonight, but I live seven miles northeast of here."

"And we live closer to where you live, David, than to this church, even though my wife and I lived in this neighborhood for the first twenty-six years of our marriage," interrupted the sixty-seven-year-old Don Becker. "Despite my affection for this community and the friends I have who still live here, I think we need to relocate to the northeast where the new housing is being built today."

"How can you say that?" challenged Harriet Wing, one of the few remaining charter members. "You know as well as I do, Don, that if we relocate, a good many of our elderly members won't be able to get out to church."

"That may be true, Harriet," replied Don, "but the future is with the young families of today, not with our generation."

"Let me make my point," pleaded David Watson. "Our charge is to choose between renovation of this old building or building a new addition next door. We were not asked to explore relocation, yet it's clear that a majority of this committee favors relocation. I think we're in trouble for going beyond our assignment!"

Two months later this futures committee, by a 7-to-1 vote, with one abstention, recommended to the membership that the Western Hills Community Church should relocate to a vacant six-acre parcel of land seven miles northeast of the present property.

The recommendation of this futures committee illustrates a point made in the previous chapter. While standing committees tend to be oriented toward yesterday and today, and also usually reinforce continuity, special study committees often work within a longer time frame, display a strong future orientation, and also feel free to go beyond their charge.

The basic generalization is that most standing committees operate under the rule that declares everything is prohibited unless it is specifically permitted. By contrast, special study committees prefer the rule that declares everything is permitted unless specifically and clearly prohibited. Since no one at the Western Hills Community Church had had the foresight to instruct the futures committee that consideration of relocation was off limits, the members of that special study committee felt free to recommend that alternative. David Watson, who abstained from that final vote, actually favored relocation. However, after eighteen years practicing a profession built around rules and boundaries, he did not feel free to recommend a course of action that clearly was beyond the charge to that futures committee.

In other words, do not be surprised if your long-range planning committee goes beyond what some believe to be the boundaries.

Grand Design or Single Issue?

The central theme of this chapter, however, is to lift up one of the big fork-in-the-road decisions often faced by long-range planning committees. Is it realistic to expect that special study committee to prepare an elaborate multi-point grand design, such as the one devised by that new pastor over at the First Presbyterian Church? Or should the expectations be more narrowly focused as they were at Western Hills Community Church where the issue was a choice among remodeling, constructing an addition to the original building, or relocating and building a new set of facilities at a new location?

This is one of scores of points at which a worshiping community is vastly different from a profit-oriented business.[2] A business can allocate a large chunk of the time, energy, creativity, and wisdom of employees to prepare a grand design or master plan for the next decade or two. Is that a fair expectation to place on five to nine lay volunteers, most of whom not only have a full-time job, but also may be carrying other volunteer responsibilities in that church and/or in denominational circles?

Is it reasonable to expect a committee of part-time volunteers to produce the same result the Reverend Jim Haines did at First Presbyterian Church? In answering that question it should be noted that Jim Haines had several advantages working for him. When he accepted that call to First Presbyterian Church, he came with the benefit of (a) a seminary education—he had been professionally trained for this vocation—(b) twenty-seven years of full-time experience in four different congregations, (c) the freedom to seek a different set of allies for every one of those nine points in his Grand Design—the ad hoc study committee normally draws all of the allies for support of each component of a multi-point strategy from within the membership of that committee and usually needs a substantial majority to support each recommendation, (d) Jim Haines worked at his job on a full-time basis while the typical long-range planning committee depends largely on part-time volunteers, (e) the only member of Jim Haines' one-person ad hoc committee that he had to win over was Jim Haines, and (f) Jim Haines carried the central responsibility *both* for designing a strategy *and* for implementing it; therefore, he needed to be acutely aware of factors such as compatibility, sequence, internal consistency, coherence, support, coordination, latent opposition, and timing. By contrast, the typical futures committee is more concerned with design and may be completely irresponsible insofar as implementation is concerned.

In addition, whenever Jim Haines saw the need to amend that Grand Design, to change the pace of implementation, to seek additional allies, or to enlist other resources, he had only to consult with himself. He did not have to call a special meeting of a committee.

Jim's wife, Betty, also recognized this fifty-two-year-old, newly arrived minister had an inner drive to prove to First Presbyterian, to Betty, to his colleagues, and to himself that he was not too old, he was not over the hill. He was still a top quality minister. Rarely does one find a committee of volunteers motivated by that kind of drive. Ad hoc study committees are more likely to be motivated by a desire to complete their assignment than by a drive to pull off a middle-sized miracle.

Incremental Change or Magic Bullet?

Another way of looking at this point is to go back to Esther Brown's comment that Jim Haines followed a strategy of incremental change. He did not expect that any one change would be decisive. His Grand Design apparently consisted of nine major strategic components plus a series of tactical points. It was a one-change-at-a-time strategy to be implemented over a long period of time.

By contrast, ad hoc committees often begin on the assumption that the world can be changed by one critical move. This concept of the magic bullet that will revolutionize the life and ministry of that congregation may be expressed in the search for a new minister or in the decision to relocate to a new site or to add a new staff person or to construct a new building or to enlarge the financial base or to adopt a specific church growth strategy.

Occasionally life is too complicated for the magic bullet to cure all ills. Are you expecting too much if you ask your ad hoc futures committee to bring in a comprehensive master plan that will cover everything from expanding the Sunday school to revitalizing the women's organization to broadening the financial base to revising the Sunday morning schedule to opening an adult day care center to creating new staff positions?

The answer is, Probably so. Do not ask an ad hoc committee of volunteers to accomplish in several months what took that experienced senior minister at First Presbyterian Church nine years to design and implement. Factors such as experience, time, role, energy, interest, expertise, and tenure suggest it may be wise to create one ad hoc study committee to bring in recommendations on expanding the teaching ministry, organize a second one to study ways of expanding the financial base of the church, ask a third committee to look into the possibilities of an Early Childhood Development Center, and look to a fourth ad hoc study group to review the Sunday morning schedule.

Do not overload any one ad hoc study committee with excessive expectations!

Exceptions and Fringe Benefits

While occasions do exist when the road to creating the grand design is the appropriate path to follow, most of the time the vast majority of congregations will be well advised to create a futures committee that is asked only to focus on a single issue. One exception may be old First Church downtown that is one-fourth the size it was three or four decades ago and needs to examine role, mission, facilities, staffing, and finances as well as programmatic concerns. A second may be the hundred-year-old ex-rural congregation that is watching the farms being replaced by shopping malls and houses. It, too, may benefit from asking one ad hoc study group to examine such issues as role, missions, priorities, location, facilities, accessibility, parking, program, and staffing. A third exception is the congregation that is experiencing the combination of the end of a twenty-year pastorate, a weak role for volunteer leadership, financial chaos, distrust, and drifting. A fourth exception may be the ex-neighborhood congregation in a community experiencing substantial demographic changes. A fifth exception may be when no full-time staff member is able and/or willing to take the responsibility for coordinating the work and intentions of various task forces or ad hoc committees that are assigned overlapping agendas. Thus the necessary internal coherence and consistency can be achieved only by giving the one ad hoc planning committee a broad agenda.

For most congregations, however, it may be more realistic to ask each ad hoc study committee to focus on only one issue. Among the fringe benefits of this approach are (1) increasing the opportunities for matching the expertise of the volunteers with that single issue, (2) opening the doors to broadening the leadership base by using five or six committees with seven members each rather than relying on one nine-member committee, (3) minimizing the risk of overloading one committee, (4) decreasing the time required for a study committee to complete its assignment, (5) reducing the chances any one group will be immobilized by an agenda that includes several divisive issues, and (6) improving the quality of the communication to the entire congregation. It is easy for one study committee to function in isolation from the ongoing policy-making standing committees, but it is far more difficult for five different ad hoc committees to completely ignore both one another plus all of those standing committees.

This raises a final question. Is it better to have several single issue ad hoc planning committees functioning concurrently or sequentially? Unless a widely perceived crisis exists, it probably will be wiser to have them function sequentially. This greatly reduces (a) the problems of coordination, (b) the chances the congregation will be overwhelmed by an excessive number of recommendations for changes, and (c) the possibilities for mutually incompatible recommendations. In addition, the sequential approach enables one ad hoc committee to build on the research, recommendations, and responses of the members to what came out of the deliberations of earlier committees.

In summary, do not expect too much from any one ad hoc planning committee. It is rare for one committee to be able to produce a grand design that will be acceptable to everyone. It is even rarer to find several ad hoc planning committees working concurrently, but separately, to produce an internally consistent grand design.

CHAPTER FOUR

Choosing a Beginning Point

WHAT ARE THE THREE CRUCIAL DECISIONS YOU FACE WHEN YOU decide to ask an ad hoc long-range planning committee to design the future for your congregation?

The first is the definition of the criteria to be used in choosing the members of this special committee. The second is to avoid the risk of extravagant expectations, a point described in the previous chapter. The third is in the choice of a beginning point or a planning model to be utilized by this committee. In most churches that choice of a beginning point will have a profound impact on the committee's agenda, priorities, discussions, and eventual recommendations. Sometimes that beginning point is defined in the charge to that special ad hoc committee, but frequently the committee chooses its own beginning point.

Six Common Beginning Points

One beginning point is to examine the range of planning models available to your committee. A widely used model is to begin by identifying all the problems confronting this congregation, giving a priority number to each one and beginning with what appear to be the most serious or urgent problems. A better model calls for identifying and affirming strengths, resources, and assets and building on these in creating that new future.[1]

Perhaps the most widely followed beginning point for planning in Protestant churches today is to use the budgeting process as a means of assigning priorities and allocating resources for tomorrow. This can be a creative approach, but the natural tendency of every allocative planning model is to cut back on expectations and to shrink the hopes and dreams for the future to fit the perceived financial limitations of today. Sometimes this cutback tendency can be curtailed by first projecting a three- or five-year program and preparing next year's budget as the first year of a long-range planning process.[2] One version of this model was described in chapter 1.

In recent years an increasingly common beginning point has been to focus on the numerical growth of a congregation and to design a planning process intended to increase growth. Sometimes the design is one that leaders hope will reverse years of numerical decline. In other cases the goal is to move this congregation up off the current plateau in size. In smaller congregations this plan usually must reflect the strengths and distinctive gifts of the minister if it is to be effective. Too often that minister moves on before the plan is implemented, and the design may not be compatible with the strengths and gifts of the successor. In larger churches that growth strategy usually must be tailored to reflect size, location, staff, facilities, resources, strengths, and the age of the members if it is to be effective.[3] (This beginning point will be explored in greater detail later in this chapter.)

A fourth beginning point is to focus on the distinctive typology or role of that particular congregation. One example is the ad hoc committee appointed to study the future of old First Church downtown. That committee might begin by visiting a half-dozen downtown churches in similar type and size cities that today are larger, stronger, and more vital than ever before in their history.[4]

Another example of this beginning point is the ex-neighborhood church that once served a walk-in constituency, but fewer than a fourth of today's members live within a mile of the building. A third example is the small town church in rural America that watches as the adult children of the older members drive ten or fifteen miles into a city church.[5] A fourth example is the twenty-five or thirty-year-old immigrant church that is discovering the children of the pioneers affirm joining an Anglo congregation as a normal and desirable part of the Americanization process. A fifth illustration is the congregation faced with the choice between continuing as a numerically declining parish at this sacred location or moving to a new site and becoming a regional church.[6]

For many long-range planning committees the beginning point was handed to the members in the decision to create it. "We are facing a crisis. We want you to study the problem and bring in an attractive solution to our crisis." The crisis may take many forms. One is that expenditures exceed income.[7] Another is what once was a beautiful and inspiring building has become a functionally obsolete structure that is expensive to maintain and tends to repel prospective new members. A third is the sudden and unexpected departure of two or three key staff members. A fourth is the growing disillusionment by the members with the policies, priorities, and pronouncements of denominational leaders. A fifth is the gradual realization that the median age of the membership is now twenty years older than it once was. Another crisis is the gradual shrinkage in the size of the crowd on Sunday morning.[8]

A sixth beginning point for the futures committee that is fairly common overlaps several of the above. This comes when the passage of time has made the historic role of that congregation obsolete.[9] One example is when the neighboring farmers sell their land to developers and that open country church meeting place in a small white frame building next to a cemetery has to redefine its role. A second is when the Swedish Lutheran parish discovers the boats no longer are coming over filled with immigrants from Sweden. A third is when a denominational merger means this church, which for decades was the only congregation of this denomination in this end of the country, is now one of seven parishes in this community affiliated with the new denomination. A fourth is when the suburban congregation founded in 1952 to reach and serve young families in a new residential subdivision discovers the median age of nearby residents is now fifty-three years, a little lower than the median age of today's members. A fifth is when the congregation that for the past thirty years has reflected the personality, gifts, theological persuasion, priorities, and skills of a devoted and hard-working minister gathers at the cemetery for a last farewell to that popular preacher. A sixth is when what once was the theologically most conservative church in town discovers that today it is just to the right of the center of the contemporary theological spectrum of churches in that community. A seventh is when the congregation averaging nearly six hundred at Sunday morning worship in 1965 felt secure in its place as the largest, most vital, strongest, best known, and most widely respected church in that small suburban community. The population has tripled since 1965, the average attendance at worship has shrunk to three hundred, what once was a vital and vibrant church now is drifting in a goalless and passive state, and it is the seventh largest Protestant church in town. In each of these, the appropriate beginning point may be a redefinition of role.

Do any of these six beginning points fit your needs? If not, keep looking for one that does. Here are a few more possibilities.

The Healthy Congregation

"The reason I'm here tonight is because I believe in preventive maintenance," declared Fred Parker, the sixty-three-year-old member who chaired the Board at Trinity Church. "Six years ago a routine physical examination revealed I had three small tumors in my colon. The surgeon removed them and the pathologist reported they were malignant, but the cancer cells had not reached the wall of the colon. If I had let it go, I might be dead now. I've had annual checkups, and each one has revealed no recurrence of the problem. Happiness is a clean colon! I also take my car in to the garage at the prescribed intervals to reduce the chances that I'll be stranded on the highway late at night."

"We're glad you have a clean colon and a healthy car," interrupted his good friend Joe Carson, "but the purpose of this meeting is not to hear a report on your colon or your car. What's your point?"

"I believe in going to the dentist when you don't have a toothache," continued Fred, "and I am recommending we appoint a special futures committee to examine the health of this congregation, to diagnose any potential problems that are still too minor to be noticeable, and to bring back to this Board any recommendations that may emerge out of their deliberations."

"I go to the dentist every six months," commented Joe Carson, "but I also don't go around kicking sleeping dogs. Why in the world should we appoint a futures committee to get people all stirred up? If it ain't broke, don't fix it, is my advice. I've been a member here for nearly thirty years now, and this church is healthier than it ever was. Last year, for the fourth year in a row, we set a new record for church attendance. We began this year with a healthy surplus in the treasury, our Sunday school is coming back faster than I ever dreamed possible, we have an excellent choir, and everybody seems to be happy. Why rock the boat?"

"I'm with Fred," asserted Linda Canseco. "I believe the best time to take a good, careful, and objective look at our future is when everything is going well. I move that Fred be asked to come to our next meeting with a list of nominees for a special futures committee."

"I second the motion," affirmed the newest member of the Board, "with the stipulation that Fred and the pastor work together in preparing that list of nominees."

"That's fine with me," agreed Linda.

Two months later this seven-member futures committee held its first meeting and agreed on a three-part planning process. Part one consisted of a diagnostic effort to identify the strengths, assets, resources, ministries, priorities, and trends that would enable them to describe contemporary reality in that parish. Part two would be to identify what they understood the Lord is calling this congregation to be and to be doing seven years hence. Part three would consist of the action steps required to transform contemporary reality into that vision of tomorrow. It should be added that the pastor was an active member of this seven-person committee with both voice and vote.

As a part of the diagnostic process that constituted the first part of this three-stage process, they sought the answers to this set of questions.

1. What has been the average worship attendance for each of the past twelve years? What does that trend line suggest?

2. During an average month, how many of our members were present on one Sunday out of four, how many on two Sundays out of those four, how many on three Sundays, how many attended all four? This required a careful survey of worship attendance covering four consecutive Sundays. What do those numbers tell us? How many visitors were present each Sunday? How many constituents who are not members, but who worship with us regularly, were present each Sunday? How many children not yet members were present each Sunday?

3. What has been the average worship attendance-to-membership ratio for each of the past twelve years? What does that tell us?

4. What has been the average attendance in the children's division of the Sunday school for each of the past dozen years? For the youth division? For the adult division? What does that tell us?

5. Which new classes were organized during the past twelve years? How is each one doing today? Why? Do we need some new adult classes?

6. How many of today's confirmed members joined during the past five years? How many during the previous five years? What proportion joined during the past five years? (A common sign of good health is that one-half of today's members joined during the past decade.)

7. What is the state of our ministry of music? How many people are involved on a continuing basis in our ministry of music? Is that number growing or shrinking? How many different music groups, both instrumental and vocal, do we have? Is that number growing or shrinking?

8. How many new members did we receive by letter or certificate of transfer during each of the past twelve years? Is that number increasing or declining? (This may be one of the best indicators of how "church shoppers" view your congregation. A reasonable goal is five or six new members, age fourteen and

over, received by letter of transfer each year for every one hundred resident members age fourteen and over.) What proportion of these new members joining by letter of transfer came from our denominational family? (While the denominational affiliation and location usually are influential variables on this indicator, if more than two-thirds of those joining by letter of transfer came from other churches of your own denomination, that suggests (a) an unusually strong dependence on denominational loyalties and/or (b) your congregation is not especially attractive to church shoppers who are shopping across denominational boundaries.)

9. How many members were lost by death during each of the past twelve years? Does that trend line tell us something? How many people were baptized here during each of the past dozen years? What does that trend line say? (A reasonable goal for many churches is that baptisms will exceed deaths by a two-to-one or three-to-one ratio, but the age mix of the membership can change that ratio substantially.)

10. How many new members were received by confirmation or by confession of faith or reaffirmation of vows or adult baptism during each of the past dozen years? What does that trend line tell us? (This number often will be a reflection of the age of today's adult members rather than an indicator of the evangelistic vitality. For example, the suburban church with many couples in their late thirties and early forties may be receiving a large number of youth as new members by confirmation. Other churches may report a large number of adult baptisms because they refuse to affirm the baptisms of other congregations.)

11. When the response to questions 8, 9, and 10 are combined with data on members removed from the roll by transfer and by action of the governing board, it will be possible to calculate the average annual losses. Most churches report they lose 4 to 8 percent of their members every year by death, transfer, or removal by action of the governing board. What is your average annual rate of losses? Why is it that low? Or that high?

12. What is the distribution of your membership by age categories? How many in each of these age cohorts: 0-13, 14-17, 18-21, 22-24, 25-34, 35-44, 45-54, 55-64, 65-74, 75-plus? Go to the library and look at the *Statistical Abstract of the United States.* This

is an annual publication of the United States Bureau of the Census and can be found in the reference department of most public libraries. Calculate the proportion of your members in each of these age cohorts. Do the same for the population of the United States or for your state. Compare the two tables.

13. Count the number of your adult (age 18 and over) members who fit into one of the following categories to determine the age and marital distribution. Calculate the percentages for each of the categories. (The numbers printed in the table below represent the distribution of the United States population, age 18 and over, in 1990.)

The percentage of resident adult (age 18 and over) members in each of these categories is

28% husbands and wives living together with children under 18 at home

32% husbands and wives living together *without* children under 18 at home

12% singled never-married men

10% single, never-married women

3% currently divorced men

5% currently divorced women

3% currently separated from spouse

1% currently widowed men

6% currently widowed women

—— Total resident adult members age 18 and over

If one spouse is a member and the other is not a member of your congregation, count the member in the appropriate category. The first two categories also include 1.8 million unmarried couples (3.6 million people) living together without children under 18 and 0.8 million unmarried couples (1.6 million adults) living together with children under 18.

How do the percentages for your adult members compare with that national pattern? (*The Statistical Abstract of the United States* can be used as a source for more recent data.)

14. What were the total receipts for this congregation for each of the past dozen years? From member contributions? From other sources (rents, interest, fees)? What does that

trend line say when compared to the inflationary rate of the past dozen years?

15. What were the total receipts from the combined contributions of your ten largest contributors last year? From the second ten? Do those totals appear to be alarmingly high? Or alarmingly low? (In congregations averaging two hundred to six hundred at worship the combined contributions of the top ten contributors often are double the combined total for the second ten.)

16. What was the indebtedness at the end of each of the last twelve fiscal years? What does that trend line suggest?

17. What proportion of the total expenditures from member giving have been allocated to missions and benevolent causes for each of the past dozen years? What does that trend line tell us? Does this congregation provide especially generous financial support for any specific mission project or cause year after year?

18. What proportion of our total annual expenditures are allocated for (a) compensation, including all fringe benefits of staff, (b) missions and benevolences, (c) care and maintenance of the meeting place, (d) program (including insurance, utilities, office supplies, materials, bulletins, music, printing, postage), and (e) capital expenditures including debt service payments? Have those proportions changed significantly during the past decade?

19. What are the assets of (a) any endowment funds, (b) a congregationally controlled foundation or trust, (c) designated reserves, or (d) other trust funds? What is the annual income from these investments? How is that allocated? Who makes those decisions?

20. In terms of ministry and program, what does this congregation do best? Second best?

21. In terms of ministerial responsibilities, what does our pastor (staff) do best? Second best?

22. Has a major event or fork in the road or change or watershed occurred since 1950 that has shaped the life of this congregation today?

23. What is the number-one "good thing" that has happened here or to this congregation during the past five years?

24. What is the distinctive appeal of this congregation to potential new members today? Is that any different from what it was fifteen years ago?

25. As we compare ourselves with other churches in this community, what is the distinctive role or identity or community image or place of this congregation today? Has that changed in any way during the past decade? If so, how? What will be the probable impact of that change for the years ahead? Does this congregation fulfill a distinctive role in terms of a particular community-wide ministry?

26. Which church was the number-one competitor with this congregation for potential new members and/or church shoppers ten years ago? Who is the number-one competitor today? If that has changed, what are the implications for the future?

27. Does this church enjoy a partnership or cooperative relationship with another congregation(s)? If yes, has that relationship changed in recent years?

28. How do our physical facilities compare with the congregation that had the best facilities fifteen years ago? Which congregation has the best meeting place (including both the buildings and off-street parking) today? Has the quality gone up?

29. As we look at our total program, both for today and at what is projected for the years ahead, does the scale of our facilities match our needs? (This may be the most complicated question on this list. One example of a problem of scale is the building that can seat six hundred for worship but can accommodate only two hundred in Sunday school and can seat only one hundred fifty at tables in the fellowship hall. A second example is the congregation that can accommodate an attendance of three hundred in Sunday school, can seat four hundred at tables in the fellowship hall, and has room for nine hundred worshipers, but the office area was designed for one pastor, one secretary, and one bookkeeper, and the largest meeting room, other than the fellowship hall, is crowded when attendance reaches twenty-five.)

Is the amount of available off-street parking adequate for weekday programming? Does a parking problem exist on Sunday morning? Can people coming to an evening activity find convenient and safe parking?

30. What improvements will we need to make to our meeting place if we are to fulfill what we believe the Lord is calling us to be and to be doing fifteen years hence?

31. Given the size, role, and style of ministry of this congregation, is it adequately staffed? If not, what are the most urgent needs? Again, this raises a question of scale and expectations. Is this congregation staffed to grow in numbers? To remain on a plateau in size? To shrink? Is it staffed to take care of the members and their children? Or to reach new generations of potential future members?

32. How many people from this congregation have gone into full-time Christian service during the past ten years? During the previous ten years?

33. Have exit interviews been conducted with staff members who left recently? If so, what was learned? If not, is it too late to do this?

34. Do you anticipate any staff changes within the next twelve months? If so, why? If so, does that create an opportunity to redefine staff responsibilities?

35. If this congregation shares a pastor with another church, is that a satisfactory arrangement? If not, what can be done to improve it?

36. What is the insurance coverage? Is this the amount and type of coverage you need today?

While this set of three dozen questions is not offered as an exhaustive list, it does provide a beginning point for the healthy congregation that wants to follow this particular three-phase planning model.[10] The first nineteen of these questions also provide an introduction to another issue that can be a serious diversion for the futures committee.

Counting Is a Prerequisite to Planning

"I don't know about the rest of you," declared Bill Jensen, a member of the long-range planning committee at Covenant Church, "but I don't want to get involved in playing a numbers game. God calls us to be faithful and obedient, and I don't think He cares about the numbers as much as He cares about whether or not we love Him and also love our neighbor. Those are the two great commandments Jesus left with us, and I think that's what we should look at."

"I'm with you, Bill," agreed Jackie Kirkwood. "The bean counters are taking over the world, and I think we need to keep them out of the church! I agree with Bill that we should concentrate our attention on quality and faithfulness. If we are faithful to God's call and do our best, the numbers will take care of themselves."

"While I'm not sure of the exact ranking, those are clearly among the five most stupid and counterproductive statements I've heard during the past twenty years," observed Sarah O'Brien, a longtime close friend of both Bill and Jackie. "As you know, I operate my own business, and we have nearly a hundred employees. Among the lessons I've learned is you can't manage what you can't count. A second lesson is numbers are an essential part of the feedback loop that enables us to take corrective action. You illustrated that on the way over here tonight, Jackie. Right after you picked me up at my house, you told me you planned to take your car to the garage tomorrow because your gas mileage has dropped. You may not like the bean counters, but what's the difference between counting beans, dollars, miles per gallon, new members received by letter of transfer, church attendance, or baptisms?"

"There's a big difference," replied Jackie. "My new car is supposed to give me good mileage. That's what I paid for. I can measure that. The church is called to be faithful and obedient. I don't know how you can measure that with statistics."

"The church also is called to baptize and win disciples to Christ," retorted Sarah, "and we can measure that. This church also exists to bring people together for the corporate worship of God and for the administration of the sacraments. I think we can measure whether we're doing that as effectively today as we did twenty years ago."

It may be useful to place this discussion in a larger historical context. The history of the origin and discovery of numbers indicates there was a time when human beings did not know how to count. Studies of preliterate societies and of early childhood development suggest that unless they can count, human beings have difficulty comprehending numbers greater than four. Only by learning to count can we discern differences in large concrete quantities. How many steps are in that staircase? If the answer is three, we can discover that with a quick glance. If the answer is fourteen, we have to count. How large was the crowd in this morning's Sunday school class? If the answer is three plus the teacher, everyone present could have told you the correct answer as they left the room without pausing for more than a couple of seconds to think about it. If the correct answer is eighty-three plus the teacher, it is unlikely anyone will be able to report that figure unless they counted.[11]

Perhaps the most interesting piece of the speculation is that the twin process of counting and recording that count may have begun seven or eight thousand years ago when the shepherd took the master's flock of sheep to the pasture. Several weeks, perhaps even months, later the shepherd returned with that flock. How could the master be sure the shepherd had been a faithful and obedient servant? Only by counting the flock before the departure and after the return to make sure none had been lost or stolen or sold.[12]

Considerable archaeological evidence exists to suggest that in Sumer, Elam, and Egypt counting and numerical notations preceded the first known forms of writing. Counting and the use of numbers clearly were and are an essential step in how human beings are able to conceptualize abstract ideas. Despite the disparaging comments about "bean counters" or "playing the numbers game," counting and the use of numbers are essential components in any system of accountability, record keeping, or planning. One outstanding example of this was the use of classes in early British Methodism and in the contemporary church in Korea as the primary means of maintaining pastoral contact and providing for group accountability. Several other religious traditions have followed the practice of dividing into two religious fellowships when the number of adults in one congregation reaches forty. That would be difficult if no one knew how to count.

More to the point, how can a futures committee plan intelligently for the future if no one knows how many people can be expected to worship God as a part of this fellowship fifteen years hence? What proportion of current receipts should be allocated for debt service if no one knows whether the indebtedness is increasing or decreasing?

In many congregations one of the first discoveries made by the members of the long-range planning committee is that no one has been counting, or that some of the reported figures are inaccurate or obsolete or do not reflect reality. In rare cases accurate counting *and reporting* is an essential component of any effort to restore people's confidence in the financial administration of that congregation. Once that trust has been broken by irresponsible actions, it may take years to rebuild it.

For a few congregations this may mean that the beginning point for the futures committee's deliberations will be to install a better quality system of record keeping and reporting. These accurate statistical records are essential for maintaining trust, for making projections about what the future may bring, and as benchmarks for subsequent congregational self-evaluation.

What Is Our Niche?

Five generalizations offer a basis for suggesting another beginning point for the futures committee. The first is that an ever shrinking proportion of churchgoers pick a church on the basis of geographical convenience. The day when one congregation drew most of its members from within walking distance of the meetinghouse has largely passed.

A second is denominational loyalties no longer are as influential as they once were in determining where people choose to go to church.[13]

A third is the increasingly common pattern for institutions to carve out a distinctive role or niche for themselves. The generalist is being replaced by the specialist. This applies to automobile mechanics, office workers, physicians, teachers, electronic data processing companies, agriculture, cable television, restaurants, banking, retail trade, and the churches.

The fourth generalization is that mature organizations usually either identify a distinctive role or watch their constituency shrink in numbers.

The last generalization overlaps these other four. It is an increasingly competitive world out there! The competition among churches today for future members is far greater than it was in 1955 when geographical proximity, inherited denominational loyalties, marriage, custom, and family pressures often determined where people went to church. In most counties with a population of 25,000 or more, the churches are faced with four choices: (a) grow older and smaller, (b) grow into a "full service" church that has the resources to offer a broad range of varied and high quality ministries and programs, (c) merge with another church to buy more time, or (d) specialize by carving out a distinctive niche.

If your congregation (a) was founded before 1965, and/or (b) averages fewer than 175 to 180 at worship, and/or (c) draws a majority of today's worshipers from beyond one mile of the meeting place, your futures committee may want to begin by asking, "What is our special role or place in this community? What do we do and do well that distinguishes us from the other churches in this community? Could it be that God has a special niche for us to fill? What are the religious needs of people that are being neglected by other churches, but to which we could offer a helpful response?"

Perhaps the most obvious example of a special niche is the congregation that reaches and serves a group of people who have strong ties to that denomination, who would not be comfortable in a church from a different tradition, and who represent the only congregation within many miles that is part of that tradition. Examples include the Seventh Day Baptist Church, the Advent Christian Church, the Friends United Meeting, and the Unitarian Universalist congregation.

A second is the congregation served by a pastor and spouse who are "home schoolers." This congregation attracts many families who also teach their children at home, rather than enrolling them in a public or private school, and who seek those weekday afternoon socialization experiences for their children.

A growing number of churches have found a special niche in a ministry with families that include a developmentally disabled child.

Back in the 1960s dozens of congregations carved out a very distinctive niche by welcoming "The Jesus People." Others became the home for a local expression of the Charismatic Renewal Movement.

Several score congregations, most of them averaging fewer than 140 people at worship, have emerged as truly racially integrated churches and identified that as their special niche.[14]

Is the identification of a special niche the logical beginning point for your long-range planning committee? If it is, you may want to skip ahead to chapter 7.

Two Beginning Points for Growth

Before returning to that popular beginning point of numerical growth that was introduced earlier, a vital distinction must be made. This is the difference between reversing several years of numerical decline and moving up off a plateau in size.

Planning to move up off a plateau in size, especially in congregations averaging fewer than 160 at worship, usually is extremely difficult. One reason is growth usually means attempting to bring strangers into a small, intimate, and warm fellowship that is reinforced by long-standing kinship and/or friendship ties. A second reason it is difficult is that substantial growth usually requires changing the basic organizing principle from a network of one-to-one relationships with the pastor at or near the hub of that network to a network of groups, organizations, classes, cells, choirs, and circles and/or to a larger and more complex program.[15]

Sometimes the move up off a plateau in size can be accomplished slowly and gradually by a "change-by-addition" strategy that leaves existing schedules, programs, groups, and classes undisturbed, but eventually that growth may require substantial changes in congregational life. The more successful that strategy is, the more likely it will mean resistance. Why? That leads to a third reason that growth is difficult for congregations on a plateau in size. One reason that congregation is on a plateau in size is because the people are content with the status quo. This absence of discontent usually produces a natural, normal, and predictable resistance to change. Why disturb those happy with the status quo?

In other words, a common beginning point in a growth strategy for the smaller congregation on a plateau in size is to expand the present package of ministries and programs. The goal is to create new entry points for potential new members.

By contrast, the beginning point in developing a strategy to reverse several years of numerical decline is even more difficult and often far more disruptive. Why?

One of the first steps in preparing this strategy is a careful and critical evaluation of what is now being done. This can be extremely threatening to several leaders since it may suggest, "You're telling us what we're doing isn't working?" The usual reason for that defensive reaction is the evaluation usually reveals that "What we've been doing isn't working." Most Christians find it difficult to discuss that evaluation in reasonably objective terms in polite, formal, and official committee meetings.

Reversing that numerical decline usually means scrapping what is not working and replacing it with the new. Change-by-replacement almost invariably is more disruptive than change-by-addition. Thus reversing the numerical decline normally is more difficult today than moving up off a plateau in size.

This replacement strategy may require replacing the present building with a new one on a different site or replacing the choir director or replacing the pastor or replacing that long-time leadership cadre that displays a high level of competence in vetoing all proposals for growth or replacing a low quality program with a high quality program or replacing an obsolete financial system with a more effective one or replacing the tradition of comforting the members with a new tradition of challenging the people or replacing the present Sunday morning schedule with a more complex one or replacing the member-oriented focus with a stronger outreach emphasis.

These examples are offered to illustrate the point that a strategy of change-by-subtraction-and-replacement usually is more disruptive than a strategy of change-by-addition and normally encounters more resistance. That also helps explain why reversing a long period of numerical decline may appear on the surface to be an attractive beginning but often is difficult to implement.

Experience suggests that (a) the greater the need for a redefinition of the role of that parish, and/or (b) the more competitive the local ecclesiastical scene, and/or (c) the longer that pattern of numerical decline has prevailed, the more critical it is for a newly arrived pastor to focus on reversing that decline during the first several months of that new pastorate. If the reversal is not underway by the end of the first eighteen months of that pastorate, it probably will not happen without radical changes. This generalization is consistent with the tradition of taking advantage of that honeymoon first year in a new pastorate.

Likewise, experience suggests that if the average attendance has dropped down into the one-hundred-fifty-to-four-hundred range, the greater the probability that an excellent match between the needs of that congregation and the gifts and skills of the new pastor can produce a quick rebound.

By contrast, reversing the numerical decline in a larger congregation often is far more complex, but it may be accomplished without a change in the pastoral leadership.

Reversing the Decline in the Large Church

"When we joined this congregation back in 1977, we averaged well over eight hundred at Sunday morning worship," recalled Bill Henry. "According to the annual report, we averaged a little over four hundred last year. It seems to me the number-one challenge before this group is to bring in recommendations that will enable us to reverse that decline."

It was the first meeting of the newly elected futures committee at Westminster Church, and it was obvious that Bill had hit a sensitive nerve. Within twenty minutes all but two members of this nine-person committee agreed that was the first question to be addressed. What is a good beginning point for a futures committee that seeks to reverse the numerical decline of what once was a very large congregation—and still is larger than nineteen out of twenty of all the Protestant congregations on the North American continent? The experiences of other large congregations suggest five alternative beginning points.

Perhaps the most widely used is to identify the distinctive assets, strengths, and resources of what is still an exceptionally large church and to decide how these might become the foundation for reaching people who currently are not actively involved in the life of any church. This beginning point usually requires an energetic, creative, and aggressive committee able and willing to be precise in its action recommendations, competent professional staff, an above average degree of internal harmony, and the absence of any divisive bickering, an attractive meeting place with above average quality meeting rooms, adequate off-street parking, a sound financial base, and a healthy, energetic, creative, vigorous, full-time minister who is willing to be an initiating leader.

A second beginning point may be to examine the quality of the meeting place, if it appears this no longer is an attractive location and/or the facilities are functionally obsolete. The possibility of relocation may be the ultimate beginning point for the final recommendation from this committee.[16] In other cases this may lead to recommendations on constructing new facilities at this site.

A third beginning point, which is the most sensitive of all, is to examine the quality of the match or fit between this senior minister and this congregation today. Sometimes it will be clear that what once was a good match is now a mismatch. In at least a few other situations, it becomes clear in retrospect that this was a mismatch from day one. Occasionally the senior minister is able and willing to adopt and implement a new and more productive approach to ministry, but that is less frequent than many hope will be true.

It is not at all uncommon for this beginning point to reveal that the issue is not the senior minister, but rather the program staff. This may be a reflection of earlier poor choices or below average compensation or of personality conflicts or simply of the fact that people do change.

The basic generalization is that occasionally the beginning

point for reversing the numerical decline of the large church is an evaluation of the staff.

For many large congregations a more useful beginning point is to ask, "What kind of large church are we?"

The large and numerically growing Protestant church of today usually can claim at least one, and often two or three or four of these five characteristics.

1. It offers exciting, rich, and attractive opportunities for Sunday morning attenders. These usually include (a) stimulating worship, (b) memorable sermons, (c) excellent adult Sunday school classes, (d) a strong children's Sunday school, (e) outstanding music, (f) an attractive and creative program staff team, and (g) convenient and easily accessible parking.

2. The most distinctive characteristic may be that array of weekday programs that report a combined weekly attendance that exceeds two thousand (one person coming on five different days or evenings counts as five). It is essential that these represent ministries of that congregation, not a landlord role in which that parish simply houses the program created by other organizations!

3. The number-one characteristic of that congregation may be the rich variety of special events and experiences week after week. These may include a six-week parenting class, a concert, a religious drama, hosting an area-wide workshop, divorce recovery events, twenty to thirty special Sunday morning worship experiences annually, guest speakers, a huge array of mutual support groups, and community-wide special Advent events that attract a couple of thousand nonmembers.

4. For a few large churches the distinctive characteristic is an exceptionally high quality ministry of pastoral care involving both paid professional staff and volunteers.

5. For others the heart of its image and role is that outstanding and widely recognized effort to challenge adults to be engaged in doing ministry both in that community and around the world.

The futures committee may ask itself, "As we seek to reverse our numerical decline, which of those alternatives will be the beginning point in strengthening, expanding, and reinforcing the ministry of this parish?"

For congregations of all sizes and shapes that are interested in numerical growth, the best beginning point may be to appoint an ad hoc committee to identify the entry points into that congregation and to bring back recommendations on how the number, variety, and attractiveness of these entry points could be enhanced.

Most long-established churches resemble a large closed circle. Most of the resources are allocated to meeting the needs of the members already within that circle. This includes the priorities on the pastor's time and energy, the use of the building, the nature of the organizational life such as the Sunday school, the ministry of music, the women's organization, the priorities in the expenditures of money, the use of the time contributed by volunteers, and the dominant approach to ministry.

If that congregation is to grow in numbers, it probably will be necessary to open several doors into that closed circle. One means of accomplishing that may be to bring in a new pastor who will introduce a new and different approach to ministry, attract new people, change the style of congregational life, alienate at least a few of the longtime members, and transform the culture of that congregation. Pastors who can accomplish that are comparatively rare! Far more often, the culture of that congregation turns out to be more powerful and molds the newly arrived minister to fit the tradition, style, ethos, approach to ministry, schedule, goals, priorities, and values of that congregation.

Rather than placing the burden on a new minister, a more productive alternative may be to open up that closed circle to potential new members by creating a series of new and attractive entry points for newcomers. Rarely is this easy! Frequently powerful pressures exist to make the number-one priority finding new members who will help perpetuate the status quo. This may be expressed as, "Before we talk about a second service on Sunday morning, let's fill all the pews at one service," or "Rather than form a new circle in our women's organization, let's try to persuade the newcomers to join those long-established circles that need new members if they're going to survive," or "Instead of talking about a new staff person to expand our program, let's first find someone who will visit our shut-ins, or who can strengthen our youth program and maybe build up our Sunday school."

One of the reasons for asking a special ad hoc study committee to focus on expanding the number of entry points, rather than turning that over to standing committees, is to avoid these diversionary pleas.

Perhaps the most subtle factor of all can be found in those smaller congregations in which the basic approach to congregational life is built on either (1) one-to-one relationships between the pastor and parishioners or (2) issue-centered ministries. Both approaches often limit the size of a congregation. In many communities, despite a sharp increase in the population of that community, those congregations remain on a plateau in size. In the vast majority of these situations numerical growth will require a greater emphasis on the group life of that congregation—and that means creating new groups for potential new members.

What Can Happen?

One ninety-seven-year-old congregation in Ohio that had been on a plateau with an average attendance of 145 at worship for the past twelve years doubled in size in five years following the arrival of a second staff member who was asked to expand the entry points. During her first year she (a) recognized that congregation was organized primarily around corporate worship and the one-to-one relationships of the pastor with individual parishioners, (b) identified a dozen volunteer allies who would help her create new entry points, (c) began to build a list of prospective new members with most of the names coming from those who attended the special events she scheduled, and (d) scheduled a total of nearly one hundred new events and activities to which nonmembers could be invited. Among other things she (1) scheduled and organized an after-church picnic for everyone in the community who had been reared in Pennsylvania with subsequent Sundays for Indiana, Michigan,

Kentucky, West Virginia, Illinois, and New York, (2) organized a four-session Divorce Recovery Workshop, (3) organized a new adult Sunday school class every year for those first five years, (4) organized a co-ed volleyball league that played three games a week in the church parking lot that first summer, (5) took that congregation out of the cooperative interchurch Vacation Bible School held in June in previous years and unilaterally organized one scheduled to be held in August, (6) enlisted a sixty-three-year-old grandmother to organize a Mother's Club for new mothers, (7) scheduled an appreciation day for all teachers employed in the local public school system for the first Sunday in September, (8) persuaded the leaders to expand the Christmas Eve schedule from one to two to eventually four services, (9) convinced the minister he should teach a new Tuesday evening Bible study group if she would recruit the members for it, (10) supported and encouraged three mothers in creating a Mothers' Morning Out cooperative child care program every Tuesday morning, (11) found a couple who could lead a series of Marriage Enrichment events, (12) identified a nonmember couple who agreed to teach a Sunday morning class for developmentally disabled people, (13) persuaded the governing board to add an early worship service to the Sunday morning schedule, (14) found someone to organize and direct a young adult choir for that new worship service, (15) talked the minister into working with a planning committee for six weeks before that first early service—and six of the nine members of that committee came from her list of prospective new members, (16) worked with two couples in organizing a Youth Club for after-school every Wednesday during the school year, (17) enlisted a member who agreed to teach a Thursday afternoon women's Bible class, (18) organized three father-daughter roller-skating Saturday afternoon events, (19) when necessary she presented her plans to the governing board as announcements rather than requests, followed by "unless, of course, the Board objects," and (20) during those first five years spent a total of $9,000 on advertising and $3,400 for outside leadership, all of which she raised outside the budget.

Of course, it is completely unrealistic to expect a committee of seven volunteers to replicate in four or five months what one full-time staff member accomplished over five years. This staff member's experience, however, does illustrate both (a) the impact of creating new entry points to attract new people and (b) the range of potential entry points in today's world.

A parallel course of action might include (a) appointment of an ad hoc study committee to examine both the need and the potential for additional entry points, (b) recommendations from this study committee on priorities, and (c) a recommendation for the addition of a part-time (or perhaps full-time) person to the program staff with a single assignment—the creation of new entry points. That study committee also would help that new staff member in identifying and enlisting the allies necessary to make this happen.

Finally, those congregations located in communities experiencing a rapid increase in the number of residents may find it wise to look at a different beginning point for that long-range planning committee. In many of these communities (a) a new congregation is launched every several months, (b) several of the long-established churches have enlarged their program staff, (c) many of the long-established congregations have expanded their physical facilities or have relocated to a larger and more attractive site and constructed a new building, (d) others have added new weekday ministries to their total program, and (e) at least a few have a new and exceptionally competent pastor.

That usually adds up to a sharp rise in the level of competition among the churches. When that happens, the beginning point for the futures committee in the long-established parish may be to review the quality of its ministry in a more competitive environment, but that requires a new chapter.

CHAPTER FIVE

The Quest for Quality

"MY VISION OF FIRST CHURCH FOR THE YEAR 2000 CALLS FOR A doubling of our worship attendance and a quadrupling of our Sunday school attendance," declared Bonnie Bonsall. The occasion was the second meeting of the recently formed long-range planning committee at the ninety-seven-year-old downtown First Church. In recent years the average attendance at worship had dropped from 350 to 240. The average attendance in the Sunday school had peaked at 466 in 1957, dropped to 275 in 1970, and to 141 in 1985. Last year it was down to 97. "I am absolutely convinced," declared Bonnie, who had joined First Church back in 1963 and also taught the high school class from 1968 to 1974, "that the key to our future is to reach a new generation of young families. The kids I taught in that high school class years ago are the parents of today's children and youth, and we're not reaching them. Of all the kids I taught during those six years that I had that class, only two are members of this church today. We need to reach that generation of parents born back in the late 1950s, the 1960s, and the early 1970s, and I am convinced the best way to do this is through a high quality Sunday school."

"That's a beautiful dream," observed Bob Gallego, "but I'm afraid it's not very realistic. We're a downtown church, our educational building was constructed in 1927, and we don't have enough off-street parking to attract those young families from the suburbs. Besides that, today's young parents want a neighborhood church."

This brief conversation raises several questions. Is the key to the future for a downtown church reaching the parents of today's children? Is Sunday school the influential factor that Bonnie Bonsall claims it is? Is it reasonable for a congregation to expect to be able to retain the allegiance of teenagers as they grow older? Is off-street parking essential for the downtown church? Do the parents of young children really prefer a neighborhood church?

These are important questions. More important, however, are two larger issues that should be on the agenda of the long-range planning of the futures committee in your church.

Age or Generation?

The first of these overlapping issues is illustrated by several long-established congregations on Florida's west coast. Back in the 1950s they attracted huge crowds every Sunday morning during the winter. Retirees came down from the North for a couple of months in the sun during January, February, and early March and stayed in downtown hotels. At several of those downtown churches one had to stand in line on Sunday morning in order to receive the ticket required for admission to the eleven o'clock worship service. The combined attendance for three services often exceeded two thousand people, and a couple of churches averaged over three thousand during the winter.

Today the number of retirees and winter visitors on Florida's west coast is several times what it was in 1957, but the February attendance at many of these churches is less than one-half what it was three or four decades earlier. What happened? The simple answer is nearly all of those retirees of 1960 either have died or are in nursing homes.

A more precise answer is in 1960 those churches attracted huge numbers of winter visitors born before 1900. The retirees and winter visitors of the 1990s are drawn largely from those generations born between 1915 and 1935. This is a new and different generation! They enjoy better health, have greater mobility, prefer to be able to choose from a wider range of alternatives, are far less willing to stand in line, take for granted a higher standard of living, and do not automatically follow in the footsteps of their parents. Many own a home in Florida and also still own a house up North.

Thus the church that attracted a large number of mature adults in 1960 may not automatically attract that same share of a similar age group thirty or forty years later.

This same point can be stated two other ways. The church or retail store or service club that depends on one specific generation of people for its clientele eventually will run out of inventory. The congregation, or denomination, that has depended on the people born before 1930 for most of its members will have many memories, but few members in the year 2010. Every congregation and every denomination must seek to reach new generations of people or eventually go out of business.

One example of this is in 1987 the mainline denominations included "45 percent of American Protestants born during the 1920s, but only 28 percent of those born during the 1960s."[1] That drop was even sharper for the Methodists. They attracted 22 percent of the Protestant churchgoers born in the 1920s, but only 11 percent of those born in the 1960s.

A second example of one religious body being successful in reaching one generation but failing to reach successive age cohorts is the Quakers. In 1750 the American colonies included 465 Congregationalist churches, 289 Anglican parishes, 250 Friends meetings, and 233 Presbyterian congregations. In terms of churches or meetings, the Quakers were the third most numerous religious group in the colonies. A century later the number of Friends meetings had increased to 350, which made them the tenth largest religious group in the United States. Lutherans had moved into first place with 16,403 parishes followed by the Methodists with 13,280 congregations, and the Baptists with 9,375 churches. Presbyterians remained in fourth place with 4,824 congregations.[2] By 1990 the Quakers had shrunk to become one of the smaller religious bodies on the American ecclesiastical scene while the Southern Baptists are second in numbers only to the Roman Catholic Church.

The same point can be made by conceptualizing your church as a passing parade of people. Most of the sixty-year-old members of 1960 are gone. Today's sixty-year-old members represent a new generation of people with a different set of expectations, priorities, values, and commitments than were carried by the sixty-year-old members of 1960.

Thus the thirty-five-year-old member of the small rural church of 1925 saw those two new outdoor toilets as an improvement over bushes and trees. The thirty-five-year-old member of that same church in 1955 agreed the time had come to install indoor plumbing.[3] Today's thirty-five-year-old new member expects the restrooms to be nearly as attractive, comfortable, and clean as the restrooms at the five-year-old shopping mall that are cleaned several times every day.

Instead of thinking in terms of age groups, it may be more productive for your long-range planning committee to focus on the generations you are seeking to reach. Instead of classifying people by age, it is more useful to recognize that generational differences do exist.[4]

What Is Acceptable Today?

This leads to one of the most widely neglected issues that deserves a place high on the agenda of your long-range planning committee. In today's world certain patterns often go together. One example is that the congregations reporting a sharp drop in the median age of the membership also usually are experiencing numerical growth. A second is that the successful efforts to reach large numbers of younger generations of members also usually are accompanied by an improvement in quality. "More" often requires "better."

It is easy for the members of a futures committee to concentrate on statistics, trends, staffing, finances, and parking, while overlooking qualitative considerations. This can be illustrated by a score of questions and suggestions that also can serve as a beginning point for the deliberations of that committee.

1. At the top of that list is the quality of the church nursery if the goal is to reach today's mothers who were born in 1955 or later.

a. Does the nursery have a wet sink so care-givers can wash their hands after changing a diaper?

b. Is it easy to disinfect the counter where the baby is placed for changing a diaper?

c. Is the nursery located on the first floor near a major entrance from the parking lot? Is it easy for a first-time visitor to find?

d. Is the nursery for babies only, not for babies and toddlers? ("I don't want a twenty-month-old boy throwing a steel truck into a crib on top of my baby!")

e. Is the nursery staffed by the same adult who is present at that same hour at least forty-five Sunday mornings a year?

f. Does the security system include giving an identification coupon or token to the parent when the baby is dropped off and require return of that identification when that baby is picked up later? (The greater the degree of anonymity, the more important is security.)

g. What is the ratio of *adult* care-givers to babies? A minimum ratio is one care-giver for each three children in the nursery. One-to-two is better and one-to-one is ideal from the parents' perspective. (Many of today's mothers will not entrust their child to a junior high care-giver.)

h. Is the room clean? Does it smell bad? Is it moldy? Are the walls clean? Is it well-lighted? Is the floor clean?

i. Are the cribs fitted with clean sheets for every baby? After each service? Or are the sheets changed only once a week? Or once every month? Or every year? Or every time someone thinks of it? Or with the arrival of every new pastor?

j. Does the nursery include rocking chairs?

k. Are the toys washed frequently?

l. Are the babies, diaper bags, and bottles clearly marked with infants' names?

m. Is a record kept of where the parents can be found in case they are needed?

n. Are the toys appropriate to the age of the babies, that is, no small pieces that they could swallow or choke on?

o. Is there a plan and clearly marked route for evacuation in case of fire?

p. Is it convenient to the place where weekday programming is held for mothers of young children?

2. Perhaps second on the quality check list is the children's

Sunday school. Do children look forward to Sunday school? What is the attendance-to-membership ratio for each class? What do parents say as they evaluate the class attended by their child? Are the rooms attractive, well-lighted, clean, and uncrowded? Are the teachers competent and well-prepared?

3. If the goal is to reach today's women and if the schedule calls for people to be in the building for a couple of hours or longer, high on this list is the women's restroom. Is there a second door between the first room (where one may come to change a diaper) and the second room with the stalls? Does each stall have a door that latches? Is the restroom cleaned daily? The more occasions where coffee is served, the more important the quality of the restrooms!

4. At least a few readers will insist that preaching should be at the top of this list—and in many churches they may be right. Outstanding preaching is often the key to reversing the long-term numerical decline of one congregation or for explaining why one new mission now averages over a thousand at worship in its sixth year and another averages eighty-five in its tenth year.

The big problem, however, is in agreeing on the definition of that term "outstanding preaching." At least ten criteria can be used in evaluating the quality of the preaching in your church.

a. Does the sermon speak to the concerns and religious needs of the people gathered in that room?

b. Does the sermon proclaim the orthodox Christian gospel?

c. Is the sermon coherent, internally consistent, and well-organized?

d. Does the sermon speak to *both* the head and the heart?

e. Will people remember that sermon a month or two later? (A persuasive argument can be made that the key word in preaching to reach people born after 1955 is "memorable.")

f. Is it motivational preaching? Will the sermons motivate people and change their lives?

g. Is it obvious the preacher believes what is being proclaimed?

h. Is everyone in the room listening and drinking in every

word? Does the delivery style of the preacher grab and hold the attention of everyone in the room?

i. Is the sermon filled with abstract concepts or is it highly visual?

j. Are the illustrations designed to evoke laughter or as a change of pace or to help listeners identify with the theme of the sermon or to make it easier for listeners to remember a central point in the sermon? (One of four deserves a grade of F, two out of four earns a B, and three out of four is required for an A.)

k. Is the delivery competitive with what television viewers see and hear in their living rooms as they watch the network newscasts?[5]

5. Perhaps the most controversial question to be raised about quality, and one of the most difficult to measure, concerns that Sunday morning worship experience. In what is increasingly a consumer-driven society, the only objective measurement is attendance.

The easiest measurement to calculate is the average attendance. Is that figure going up or down?

A better yardstick is to examine the frequency of attendance. How many members attend at least forty-five Sundays a year? How many attend at least forty Sundays a year? Are those numbers going up or down?

Today, as never before in American church history, people believe they have a right to choose where they worship. Family ties, habit, denominational loyalties, tradition, geographical proximity, and personal convenience are less influential than they used to be in determining where people go to church. Increasingly the crucial variable is, Are my religious needs being met in this church? One example of this is the growing numbers of adults who fulfill their need for a caring Christian community by attending an adult Sunday school class in Church A where they have been members for many years, but now go to Church B for corporate worship to have their spiritual cup filled.

This leads to a third criterion for worship. Are your members so enthusiastic about the worship experience in your church that they invite their friends, neighbors, kinfolk, and colleagues at work, "Come to my church with me next Sunday"? While this is a more subjective yardstick than counting the attendance, it may be the best indicator of quality. How many of your members bring a nonmember to worship on the average Sunday?

6. For some readers the most divisive issue on this list is music. How do you rate the quality of your music ministry? What are the criteria? Which generation(s) are you seeking to reach through your ministry of music? Do you design the early Sunday morning worship experience to satisfy the preferences of one group for a particular type of music and design the second service to reach a different audience?

7. High on this list is the quality of the space set aside for the corporate worship of God and the administration of the sacraments or ordinances.

The second floor sanctuary no longer is as acceptable as it was in 1910 when the average life expectancy for American men was fifty years and fifty-four for American women. Those flights of stairs are less of a challenge to fifty-year-olds than they are to seventy-five-year-olds.

Lighting, acoustics, design, exits, placement of the choir, and decor are other criteria for evaluating the quality of your place of worship.

8. As was pointed out earlier, the comparison base for evaluating restrooms today is the shopping mall, not the rural church of 1940. This is especially important if the goal is to reach women in general and especially the mothers of young children.

9. If the goal is to reach the generations born after 1940, high on this search for quality is the teaching ministry. This includes the Sunday school, adult Bible study classes, and what happens during the worship service. Many church shoppers born after 1955 point to the teaching during that 75-to-100-minute worship service on Sunday morning or Sunday evening as the number-one reason they picked this particular church.

10. The smaller the size of that worshiping community, the greater the weight that must be given to the quality of the fellowship and the friendliness as perceived by first-time visitors. An extroverted, gregarious, cheerful, outgoing, friendly, and

smiling pastor can be a tremendous asset in modeling friendliness. That is true regardless of the size of the congregation.

The larger the size of the crowd on Sunday morning, the more influential the physical facilities will be in determining whether or not a first-time visitor perceives this to be a "friendly church.

Most houses of worship were designed to facilitate the evacuation of the crowd in case of fire. A few, however, were designed to encourage people to linger, talk, and enjoy one another's company. In these buildings the space for those coming to or departing from worship is through a large room designed to discourage a quick exit and to encourage conversation.

A parallel point is that in most houses of worship corridors and stairways were designed to facilitate pedestrian traffic. In a few, however, they were designed to enhance fellowship and interpersonal relationships.

Was your building designed to encourage or discourage conversation and fellowship? Was it designed to be functional or to enhance relationships?[6] If you are dissatisfied with it, what is your most attractive alternative course of action?

11. Overlapping several items on this list is the quality of the process for the assimilation of newcomers.[7] How many first-time visitors return the following week? What proportion of the members who joined two years ago are active today? What proportion of your leaders come from among the recent new members?

12. Perhaps the least studied facet of quality is community image. How do nonmembers, and non-churchgoers in particular, view this congregation? What is the image outsiders have of this church? Is it favorable? Is it obsolete? Is it what you want it to be? What are you going to do to strengthen that image?

13. Perhaps the most paradoxical item on this check list is the quality of the financial administration. If it is precise, accurate, up-to-date, and lucid, that will do little to strengthen the life and ministry of your congregation. People expect it will be perfect. The parallel is that few people notice when the sun rises in the east. It is only when the sun rises in the west that people become agitated, excited, and upset.

Few people applaud an excellent system for administering and reporting the finances of a worshiping community. When, however, it is discovered that funds are misappropriated or when money contributed for missions is spent on operating expenses or when the reporting system is inaccurate, incomprehensible, non-existent, or several months behind schedule, people become disturbed. Not only is their trust undermined, many find the most attractive course of action is to silently disappear.

14. Overlapping that is the quality of internal communication. The increased competition for the eye, ear, and mind of today's adult means every church has to work harder than ever to maintain an adequate two-way system of communication. Some of this can be accomplished through videotapes, newsletters, special mailings, meetings, posters, the grapevine, telephone calls, radio, the local newspaper, announcements in the bulletin, and fellowship occasions, but part of it can be done only through one-to-one communication.

One of the consequences of inadequate internal communication is low morale, another is a decrease in the frequency of attendance, and a third is a dropoff in activity. The easiest-to-measure consequence is a decrease in the level of financial support. The most serious, however, is the number of members who quietly disappear as a result of inadequate internal communication.

15. Back in the 1860 to 1960 era many Protestant congregations thrived by building a strong network of "lay-owned" and "lay-operated" organizations. The two outstanding examples of this were the Sunday school and the women's organization. In some congregations that list was supplemented by a men's fellowship, a youth group, a missions organization, the ministry of music, a Scout troop, and perhaps athletic teams. The central role of lay volunteers made it possible for relatively large congregations to function effectively with a small paid staff.

If your congregation places a premium on the organizational life, you may want to ask these six questions:

a. What is the health and vitality of each of these organizations today?

b. Which ones are growing younger (in terms of the age of

the participants) and larger? Which ones are growing older and smaller? Why?

c. What proportion of the leaders in each organization united with your congregation during the past five years?

d. How many new groups, circles, cells, choirs, classes, or sub-units have been created by each organization during the past three years?

e. Are these organizations attractive entry points for potential future members of this organization?

f. Which of these organizations are largely or entirely staffed by volunteers and which ones are heavily dependent on paid staff?

16. The number-one strength of some congregations is the pastoral care of the members. If the pastor excels in this, the members find it easy to forgive uninspired or incomprehensible sermons, a weak teaching ministry, or poor administration.

What is the quality of the pastoral care of your people? How can it be improved? What is your comparison base? With five years ago? Or with another congregation that excels in pastoral care?

17. For the past four decades a growing number of congregations have replaced that earlier emphasis on lay-owned and lay-led organizations with a new focus on small face-to-face groups. Is this a high priority in your parish? If it is, what is the vitality of the group life? What proportion of today's members are actively involved in a small group week after week? How does that proportion compare with five years ago? With ten years ago? Are these groups effective entry points for new people coming into your congregation? How many new groups were created last year? How many of those created two years ago still exist? Or is the emphasis on building a few high quality groups rather than on reaching a larger proportion of your people?

18. For many parents the first question to ask when the issue of quality arises is, "Why doesn't our youth group attract more teenagers?"

Perhaps the most common explanation is that the current youth program was designed to reach the generation born in the 1942–55 era or the generation born in the 1956–69 period, and that design is now obsolete. Most of today's teenagers were born long after 1969.[8]

Three of the critical questions to ask on this are, (a) Was the youth program designed to reach small numbers or large numbers of teenagers? (b) Was it designed to reach today's generation of teenagers? (c) Was it designed to reflect the learnings gleaned from "family systems theory"[9] or was it designed to isolate the youth from that family context?

This, incidentally, may be the most difficult assignment to give to a committee of volunteers seeking to evaluate the life and ministry of their parish.

19. Readers west of the Mississippi River or those in congregations seeking to reach the generations born after 1955 may want to move this next subject to the top of their agenda in congregational self-evaluation.

That subject is attractive, easily accessible, visible, and adequate off-street parking.

The two key guidelines are (a) few people will walk more than 1,200 feet to worship with you on Sunday morning, even fewer will walk 600 feet to attend an after-dark meeting, and (b) the definition of "adequate" is three spaces are still vacant six minutes after the beginning of the most heavily attended worship service on Sunday morning.

20. One of the most difficult and highly subjective assignments in congregational evaluation is the staff. This requires looking at a long list of criteria including (a) the quality of the "match" between the staff member and this congregation, (b) productivity, (c) creativity, (d) personality, (e) technical competence, (f) the ratio of staff-to-worship attendance,[10] (g) compatibility of staff members with one another, (h) the model of staff relationships, (i) tenure, (j) experience, (k) compensation, (l) age, (m) education, and (n) the expectations placed on each member.

For those congregations averaging more than seven hundred at worship, the most critical single variable in determining whether that parish will experience numerical growth or decline usually is not location or physical facilities or denominational label or local population trends or age of the membership. The crucial variable usually is staff. In other words, the larger the congregation, the more important is a high quality program staff.

21. Finally, if the search for quality is chosen as the beginning point for the deliberations of your long-range planning committee, that effort should include a review of the place of missions and community outreach. While this subject merits a separate book, six evaluative questions offer a beginning point.

a. What proportion of the total amount of money contributed annually each year is allocated to missions and benevolences? (For purposes of comparability, this should include contributions to finance the operations of the denominational offices, theological seminaries, and interchurch agencies as well as that which goes for "missions.")

For most denominationally related churches 10 percent should be seen as an absolute minimum simply to carry a "fair share" of the cost of denominational operations. A figure of 15 or 16 percent is "average," 20 percent is good, and 30 to 35 percent earns a grade of "excellent."

b. Has that percentage been going up or down in recent years?

c. How many of your members were actively involved last year as volunteers in feeding the hungry, calling on the sick and the shut-ins, sheltering the homeless, visiting those in jail or prison, helping start a new church, repairing the damage after a natural disaster, and similar acts of Christian mercy?

d. Has that number or proportion been increasing in recent years?

e. Does your congregation have an *earned* reputation as an advocate of social justice?

f. How many of your members visited or worked in a mission field outside your state last year?

In one respect the answers to these questions parallel the quality concerns raised earlier on financial administration and good internal communication. A grade of "A" on any one or all twenty of these questions may not have an obvious positive impact on the life, morale, and vitality of your congregation, but a grade of "D" can undercut morale, self-esteem, vitality, and health!

This quest for quality can be an especially useful beginning point for the newly appointed futures committee in (1) the suburban congregation that is in a far more competitive ecclesiastical environment than it was in 1955 or (2) in old First Church downtown or (3) in the county seat church that is intentionally extending the radius of its service area from two or three to fifteen or twenty miles or (4) in the parish that is redefining its role from a neighborhood church to a regional church.

For others a useful beginning point is to count the votes people cast with their feet or their pocketbooks.

CHAPTER SIX

Reading the Election Returns

"SOME OF YOU MAY STILL BE WONDERING WHY THIS COMMITTEE was created so soon after my arrival," explained Terry Hudson, the new senior minister at First Church. Terry had arrived in late June, and this first meeting of the newly created futures committee was being held on a hot Tuesday evening in early August.

"Three weeks ago I asked the Church Council to authorize the creation of this group, and we picked the membership that same evening," continued this forty-three-year-old senior minister who was willing to accept the role of an initiating leader. "When a couple of council members questioned the need to act so quickly, I offered five reasons. First, as some of you are aware, the treasurer reported that we were coming into the summer months with a severe cash flow problem. Our expenditures for January through June are nearly $35,000 greater than our income. That was the first piece of bad news that I received the day we moved here. One of our assignments is to devise a plan we can implement in September to wipe out that deficit."

"I know we're running a deficit," interrupted Hazel Moore, who had joined First Church in 1959, "and I agree we need to do something about it beyond scolding that loyal core who show up every Sunday morning, but I believe a more important issue is to discover why we're running a deficit."

"You're absolutely right!" agreed this new minister, "and that's the most critical reason for creating this committee. I'm new here, and I need your help in interpreting the data we have. Before we moved here, I received a huge packet of information in response to a bunch of questions I asked, and I want you to help me understand what all those facts and figures mean. I agree with Hazel. Churchgoers do vote with their feet and their pocketbooks. For example, I see that average attendance at worship has dropped from over eight hundred ten years ago to six hundred two years ago to a shade over five hundred last year. My hunch is that is a big reason behind the financial squeeze."

"We don't need a special committee to explain that," suggested Robin Grieve. "I think everyone in this room will agree that attendance began to drop soon after the arrival of your predecessor nine years ago. He was simply a boring preacher who read his sermons in a monotone. Some of us wondered how he was able to stay awake when we couldn't."

"I've been told that before," observed the Reverend Terry Hudson, "but why did it drop so slowly? If people vote with their feet and their pocketbooks, why was the decline so gradual? This is the second reason for this committee. I want you to help me interpret the election returns."

"I can give you four big reasons why we didn't experience a total exodus," explained Jack Johnson. "First, we have eight loyal adult Sunday school classes. Most of the members of those classes found it almost impossible to leave. Second, we have a superb ministry of music with six different music groups including the best chancel choir in town. Third, a bunch of us have been members of First Church for at least twenty years, and we're not about to leave because of a mismatch between pastor and congregation. Fourth, you also should know, Terry, that while your predecessor was a boring preacher, he was the best minister I've ever known in one-to-one relationships, he loved the flock, he was a great pastor in a time of crisis, he was a hard-working minister who rarely took a day off, and he believed in calling on people in their homes. Those characteristics did not fully offset his shortcomings in the pulpit or as an administrator, but I think we would all agree he was a dedicated man of God."

"You bet he was!" added Pat McGuire. "When our seventeen-year-old son was killed in an automobile accident four years ago, he was waiting for us when we arrived at the hospital at one o'clock that Saturday morning. No minister could have been of greater help to me and our family than he was. You may think his sermons were boring, but his love was genuine!"

"I didn't say his sermons were boring," declared Robin Grieve defensively. "He had some excellent content in those sermons, and they were carefully prepared. What a lot of the people complained about was his delivery. The content was good, but the delivery could have been improved."

"It was primarily a mismatch," observed Hazel Moore. "He really belonged in a small county seat church where his personal qualities would have fit better. A big church like this one needs a senior minister who is a top flight pulpiteer, an excellent administrator, a strong leader, and also is comfortable working with large groups of people."

"Your reflections are interesting and useful," interrupted the new senior minister, "but this committee was not organized to conduct a post-mortem on my predecessor's ministry, but rather to help shape the future. That brings me to the third reason I asked for your help. As a general rule, the larger the congregation, the more important it is for a new minister to make the best use of that honeymoon first year. I need your help in shaping the future of this congregation. What do you believe God is calling this congregation to be and to be about five years from now?

"A fourth reason," continued Terry while ignoring those who wanted to comment on what the future should bring, "is our annual meeting is scheduled for five months from tomorrow night. I need your help in preparing some short-term goals for next year.

"Finally, the fifth reason I asked for this committee is that I need your help in understanding the local context. I go on the assumption that every church is different from all other congregations and also every community provides a unique context for doing ministry. I need to learn more about the distinctive culture of this congregation as quickly as possible. Three of you have been members of First Church for more than a quarter century, and that can be of great value to me."

"Maybe I shouldn't be on this committee," ventured the

twenty-six-year-old Shelly Warren somewhat timidly. "I'm not even a member. We moved here last April and began attending the first Sunday after we arrived, but we haven't joined yet."

"That's why you were asked to serve," assured Terry. "I asked that someone be named who was new to this community, new to this church, and under thirty years of age. Everyone on the Church Council agreed you would be the ideal choice."

Can This Be a Useful Beginning Point?

This conversation introduces what can be an exceptionally productive beginning point for an ad hoc long-range planning committee. This is shortly after the arrival of a new pastor. This is most likely to be a useful beginning point if all four of the following conditions prevail.

First, and by far the most critical, is whether the newly arrived minister wants the assistance of such a committee. If that new pastor does not want it, forget it! A fair number of pastors take very seriously that ancient bit of advice, "Don't rock the boat in your first year. Use that first year to learn the lay of the land and to discover the influential leaders." That is wise advice in perhaps one-fourth to one-third of all new pastorates, especially in smaller churches, in rural congregations, in those situations where the predecessor was forced to leave or when the termination was an unusually disruptive or diversionary experience for that worshiping community. In at least two-thirds of all new pastorates, however, the creation of an ad hoc futures committee can be a highly productive course of action.

Second, an openness to change and innovation usually is a valuable part of the congregational context. If everyone hopes the new minister will be a carbon copy of the predecessor, only better, it may be wise to wait a year or two or three before creating a futures committee. Planning for change usually can be accomplished more readily if supported by discontent with the status quo.

In other words, the more widespread the discontent with the status quo, the more likely a special ad hoc study committee will have a receptive audience for its recommendations during that honeymoon year.

To be more specific, if the trend lines on membership, worship, attendance, baptisms, Sunday school attendance, financial contributions, mission support, and new members received have been down for the past few years, this usually creates a greater openness to change and new ideas than if those trend lines reflect a comfortable plateau in size. (It should be noted that changes in the number of baptisms often reflect the changing age mix of the membership more than any changes in evangelistic fervor.)

Third, widespread agreement on the basic facts is extremely important. This is largely a product of the quality of the record keeping and the reporting. It is amazing how often members are in sharp disagreement over relatively objective questions. Has our attendance been going up or down? One's perception of that trend may depend on whether one attends the early service or the late service. Are we growing older or younger? Again the perception may vary depending on one's point of involvement. Is member giving going up or down? A decrease may have been concealed by an increase in rental income or in bequests or in user fees or the contributions of one or two extremely generous new members.

The better the quality of the records, the easier it is to study and learn from looking at how people vote with their feet and their pocketbooks.

Finally, the larger the number of new members who have united with this congregation in recent years, the stronger the future orientation. If one-half or more of today's members have been members for fifteen years or longer, this may reinforce a strong past orientation. If, however, more than one-half of today's members joined during the past eight or nine years, it is far more likely the congregation will display a powerful future orientation. The stronger the future orientation, the more supportive will the congregational climate be for that futures committee's deliberations.

As a general rule, the larger the average attendance at worship, the more receptive the congregation will be to a new pastor who is an initiating leader and wants to reap every possible benefit from that honeymoon year. Thus the congregation averaging around three hundred at worship probably will be twice as receptive to that style of leadership as will the congregation averaging one hundred fifty at worship.

Likewise, if the election returns reveal that congregation is in a declining state, the receptivity to change will be greater than if the congregation has been on a comfortable plateau in size for years.

For many congregations a careful analysis of the election returns will lead to the conclusion that the time has come to redefine the role of that parish and to carve out a new niche for the years ahead. Can a study of these numbers be a useful beginning point for your long-range planning committee?

CHAPTER SEVEN

Carving Out a Niche

FOR MORE THAN THREE HUNDRED YEARS PROTESTANT CHURCHES on the North American continent enjoyed four powerful advantages in attracting generation after generation of replacement members. For many churches the most powerful of these was kinship ties. The adult children tended to become members either of (a) the congregation into which they had been born or (b) the congregation into which their spouse had been born.

A second powerful motivating factor in deciding where a person worshiped was denominational loyalty. Institutional loyalties in general and denominational loyalties tended to be passed from generation to generation and from sibling to sibling.

As recently as 1952, for example, four out of five adult churchgoers who identified themselves as Baptists, Methodists, or Lutherans also reported they had been members of that same denominational family for all of their life or had married into it from an unchurched background.[1] The proportions were seven out of ten for Episcopalians, Congregationalists, and Presbyterians. Nine out of ten Roman Catholics either had been born into a Catholic family or had married a Catholic.

Most adult Christians on this continent either continued in the congregation in which their parents had been members or, if they moved, they stayed in that same denominational family when they sought a new church home. The dominance of denominationally affiliated churches began to erode in the 1950s and was accompanied by a rapid increase in the proportion of younger adults who chose an independent or nondenominational parish.

This combination of kinship ties and denominational loyalties clearly was a factor in the numerical growth of several of the old-line denominations during the 1946–65 era.

A third factor, which began to diminish in importance with the generations born after 1935, was a nationality heritage. This appeared to be the number-one attraction in thousands of congregations, both Catholic and Protestant, that had been created to reach the people whose ancestors had been born in England, Germany, Holland, Scotland, Wales, Africa, Denmark, Sweden, Finland, Norway, Bohemia, Italy, Poland, Mexico, Japan, France, Romania, or some other land.[2]

The last of these four factors that had such a powerful influence on where people went to church was geography. A three-mile radius for the service area of a parish meant it took some people an hour each way to go to church and to return home.

The Importance of That Third Place

When combined together, these four factors made church "a home away from home" for many of the more active members. It was what Ray Oldenburg has described as "the third place."[3] By definition "a third place" is the gathering spot that is separate from the place of work and from the home where a person can meet others who are not a part of one's immediate family and also are not encountered in the place of work. Historically, the third place has been within walking distance of both home and the place of work. For many men, this was the neighborhood bar. (The number of neighborhood bars shrunk by two-thirds between 1950 and 1990.) For millions of farm wives and children this was the general store. For village residents, it may have been the post office. For thousands of farmers it was the hardware store or the blacksmith's shop. For teenagers it may have been the soda fountain or, in the 1950s, the drive-in hamburger shop. For millions of women it was the monthly meeting of the Ladies Aid or the Missionary Society. For farm children it may have been the regular meeting of the 4-H Club at someone's home. For some city youth it was the public library or a local playground. For thousands of men the third place was the lodge hall or veterans' building or "The Club."

For many churchgoers of all ages it was the church. Sometimes that was an adult Sunday school class. Sometimes it was the Sunday evening service or Wednesday evening prayer meeting.

This was the place you could come and be valued as a person, not as an object, where one could be with those who shared a common value system, and a common perspective on life and where everyone spoke the same language. This was the place where socializing, silence, caring, concern for one another, loitering, small talk, patience, gossip, lingering, and a strong past orientation were valued as social assets, not liabilities to upward mobility. Conversation, camaraderie, sharing, and philosophizing were critical ingredients of the traditional third place. The third place was less of a place to meet and make new friends and more of an opportunity to reinforce old friendships or to turn acquaintanceships into friendships.

For millions of families the white frame church out in the open country was the third place. For many villages it was the small brick church a block or two removed from the road that ran through the middle of that community. For others it was the lodge hall or the bridge club or the threshing ring or the pool hall or the service club.

For a few adults today the tailgate party in the parking lot before the football game has become a cherished third place. For millions of people born after 1945 that third place is a favorite restaurant or private club or an adult Sunday school class or a car pool or a bar or a playground or a beauty parlor or someone's house.

Oldenburg argues, however, that for an ever-growing proportion of the population the third place does not exist. He points out that in the country store or the neighborhood bar socializing was given a higher rank than merchandising. In today's enclosed shopping mall, which may be the third place for some early morning mature mall walkers and for many more after-school teenagers, merchandising, not socializing, is the dominant theme of that social setting.

Oldenburg also has pointed out that the larger the circle of one's friends and acquaintances, the less chance of the marriage ending in divorce. Sometimes the excessive expectations placed on a marriage and/or on that nuclear family can undermine family relationships. A healthy third place can reduce some of those pressures.

In recent decades television has offered viewers the vicarious opportunity to visit a third place without leaving their living room. Concurrently, the divorce rate has nearly doubled and more people complain about "stress" and "burnout." Is that a coincidence?

Historically, third places have provided people the opportunity to improve their skills in interpersonal relationships, to "blow off steam" without offending spouse or children, to enjoy a change of pace for an hour or two, to hear some sage advice delivered in a non-threatening setting, to look at the world from another perspective, and to be socialized into a society that extends beyond work and family.

For millions of American Protestants their church filled that need for a third place. Does your church fill that role for many of your people today? Or is that yesterday's role?

To Do or to Be?

It is easy to oversimplify life. It is equally tempting to romanticize the past. Given these two limitations, however, it may not be too much of an exaggeration to suggest the first places of life are filled with expectations about doing. Breadwinner, parent, spouse, child, worker, employee, cook, homemaker, farmer, or entrepreneur all carry implications about doing. The dominant theme of "the great good places" (to use the title of Oldenburg' s book) are primarily places of being. Your identity is in who you are as a person, not in what you do.

In many of today's larger Protestant congregations the highly structured program is built around doing. A person comes to worship God, to sing in the choir, to work in the kitchen, to serve on a committee, to teach in the Sunday school, to chair a special task force, to count money, to help paint a room, to stuff envelopes, to chaperone an outing with the youth, to decorate the sanctuary for Advent, to study the Bible, to listen to a lecture, to usher, to fill a vacant chair, or to direct a children's choir. In the best of the larger churches emphasis on doing is tempered with a separate layer of relational or mutual support groups organized around being, not doing.[4] Rarely, however, are as many as 60 percent of the adult members actively involved in one of these relational groups on a continuing basis. More frequently, that proportion is less than one-third and some of these groups strike the first-time visitor as more concerned with doing than with being.

This discussion provides a context for your long-range planning committee to look at the carving out of a distinctive niche as a possible beginning point in its deliberations. This is especially relevant if your congregation averages fewer than two hundred at worship. Before opening that door, however, it may be useful to quickly review a few contemporary trends.

Eight Influential Changes

The first of these, as was mentioned earlier, has been the gradual disappearance of the language and nationality ties that were such a powerful cohesive force for thousands of parishes between 1840 and 1960. The self-identified "American" succeeded the German-American, the Hollander, the Italian-American, the Mexican-American, the Japanese-American, and the Swedish-American.

A second trend has been the lowering of the denominational barriers. In 1965 6 percent of all Lutherans identified themselves as former Methodists compared to 3 percent in 1952. Ten percent of all Episcopalians identified themselves as former Presbyterians in 1965 contrasted to only 3 percent thirteen years earlier. In 1965, 8 percent of all Presbyterians were former Baptists compared to only 4 percent in 1952.

The third trend is that tiny stream of Roman Catholics coming into Protestant churches has begun to grow. In 1952 only 4 percent of all Lutherans, 1 percent of all Presbyterians, Congregationalists, and Episcopalians, and 2 percent of all Methodists identified themselves as former Catholics. By 1965 those percentages had climbed to 8, 5, 4, 6, and 3 respectively.[5] Research by Catholic scholars suggests that by 1989 at least six million of the baptized souls carried on the rolls of Roman Catholic parishes had left to join a Protestant worshiping community.

By 1985 the number of people switching religious affiliation had climbed steeply. At least one-third of the adults born after World War II had left the denominational family in which they had been reared.[6]

A fourth trend is those churches that relied heavily on kinship ties or on denominational loyalties as a source for numerical growth began to experience a decline in numbers back in the mid-1960s. This was clearly a factor in (a) the decline in Sunday school attendance since younger families with children were going elsewhere and (b) the aging of the membership—the death rate among members of The Methodist Church in 1952, for example, was 8.9 per 1,000 members, well below the 11.4 figure for the American population age 14 and over. By 1989 the death rate in The United Methodist Church was 13.5, well above the rate for the American population age 14 and over, which had dropped to 10.6 per 1,000 persons. A similar pattern in the aging of the membership can be seen in several other old-line denominations.[7]

This trend was reinforced by a number of denominational mergers—which tend to erode denominational loyalties—and the emergence of a new generation of adults who, as a group, tended to be less interested in inherited institutional loyalties. (This also has produced big problems for lodges, political parties, private colleges, scouting, and service clubs.)

A fifth trend that is less widely discussed is the increase in the average size of Protestant congregations. Between 1906 and 1986 the average size of Protestant congregations in the United States tripled. Kinship ties and denominational loyalties are less powerful attractions to potential future members for the big churches. In these parishes preaching, program, and quality are far more influential forces in attracting new generations of people.

A sixth trend has been that the costs of providing person-centered services—as contrasted with the costs of producing things such as ballpoint pens, typewriters, tires, wheat, coal, timber, or radios—has increased more rapidly than the increase in people's incomes. Labor intensive services such as a day in a hospital or a day in court or an hour in worship or a day in a third-grade classroom or a visit to a physician or an hour with a counselor or the repair of an automobile engine or the response to a call by the fire department cost more today than they did in 1960, after allowing for the impact of inflation.

A seventh significant trend was discussed in chapter 5. Today people are more insistent on quality than their parents were in 1952. People are willing to pay more for quality, they are willing to travel greater distances to get it, and they will make sacrifices in order to receive higher quality. This can be illustrated by single family homes, medical care, vacations, music in church, children's education, automobiles, motels, shopping malls, and public transportation. (In 1970 domestic airlines carried fewer passengers than traveled by inter-city bus. In 1985 domestic airlines carried four times as many passengers as inter-city buses.)

Finally, the adults of today, unlike their parents, are less likely to be influenced by inherited loyalties and more likely to disregard traditions when making a choice of schooling, job, place of residence, church, or when confronted with a choice among historic brand names versus generic products of new labels. The higher a person is on the educational or the income scale, the more likely that generalization will hold.

What Does This Mean?

Perhaps the most highly visible implication of this combination of trends is that those churches that were heavily dependent on kinship ties and denominational loyalties to produce a new generation of members have been hurting. This is most apparent among a half-dozen old-line Protestant denominations, but also can be seen in the Roman Catholic Church.

Less visible, but more serious, has been the impact on thousands of small congregations in large central cities and in rural America. In both places thousands of churches have closed. In addition to the erosion of kinship and denominational ties, these churches also have been hurt by the exodus of the Anglo population whose ancestors came from northern Europe, by the decision of the children to seek greener pastures, by that new emphasis on quality and the willingness to travel a long distance for it, by the preferences of people born since 1945 for large congregations with a broader range of programming, and by rising costs. (Caution! The much discussed mobility of the people as a factor may be overstated since 54 percent of all Americans live within fifty miles of where they were born. In 1880, 78 percent of the native-born population lived in the state in which they had been born. By 1960 that proportion had dropped to 74 percent, and today it is about 69 percent.)

Like hospitals, automobile manufacturers, private colleges, dentists, radio station owners, grocery stores, physicians, and magazine publishers, the old-line Protestant denominations and the long-established congregations built around that combination of a denominational label—a common nationality heritage and kinship ties—are discovering this is a highly competitive world today. This has been especially hard on smaller congregations.

A second implication is in church finances. For better or for worse, the teachings on stewardship have been effective, and an increasing proportion of church members are convinced they must be faithful stewards of what God has given them. Formerly they gave to congregational and denominational causes out of loyalty. Today many feel an obligation to be responsible stewards in deciding where their charitable contributions should go. One result is that an increasing number of denominations and church-related institutions are making financial appeals to individuals rather than expecting that money to flow through congregational and/or regional judicatory channels.

Many will argue that the most significant implication is in new church development. In the 1950s it was widely assumed that new churches would be organized "to serve our people who are moving out there." Today, except for parts of the South, denominational loyalties are a minor factor in determining who the first two hundred members will be in that new mission.

Leaders from numerically growing smaller congregations contend that the primary reason they are increasing in numbers is that they no longer depend on kinship ties as a source of replacement members but have decided to concentrate on meeting the religious needs of a new generation of adults.

Some of the more critical commentators on these trends insist that the most serious implication is what they label "consumerism." The kinship ties and/or denominational loyalties that once kept members from dropping out have been replaced by a self-centered stance that frees many people to leave the church they were reared in to go in search of a religious congregation that will meet their spiritual needs. Followers of Martin Luther, Menno Simons, Huldreich Zwingli, John Calvin, Count Nicholas von Zinzendorf, or John Wesley might insist that is not a new development. Whether it be labeled "consumerism" or a religious pilgrimage, the erosion of kinship ties has strengthened that sense of freedom to seek out the church that meets one's own religious needs.

Is the power of kinship ties a cohesive force in your congregation today as it was in 1924 or 1954? If not, what are the new cohesive forces that bind your members together?

Seven Alternatives

One effective response to that erosion of nationality, denominational, and kinship ties is to make your church an attractive "third place." This is easiest to accomplish if (a) the turnover in the local population is relatively low, (b) your church enjoys pastorates that typically range between fifteen and thirty years in length, (c) your congregation includes fewer than two hundred members, (d) the design and location of your meeting place can enable it to become an attractive third place, and, most critical, (e) your pastor is both able *and* willing to help make this happen.

Dozens of relatively small ex-neighborhood churches in large central cities have become that third place for single adults in their twenties and thirties who moved from smaller communities to the big city in search of a job or career. This also requires a personable, creative, and long-tenured pastor with a high level of skill in integrating newcomers into a long-established institution. It can happen, but it is rare.

A second alternative that may have peaked in popularity in the 1960s is that each congregation should represent a specific and clearly defined ideological position.[8] Ideology, rather than relationships or functions, should be the primary source of identity. This choice is easiest to implement in a new and theologically conservative congregation in which the founding minister is still the pastor. It is a far more difficult-to-implement alternative in theologically liberal congregations because of the divisive nature of the issues that cannot be ignored.[9] Perhaps the most divisive issue for an ideological congregation to grapple with today is pornography.[10] It often is nearly as difficult to secure a widely agreed upon definition of social justice[11] to rally broad support for a particular position on taxes or on financing health care for every citizen or on television or abortion or homosexuality or American foreign policy or church-state relationships or on the merits of a strong denominational affiliation.

A third alternative is to merge with another congregation, but all too often the arithmetic of that has meant the 150-member congregation merged with the 180-member church to produce a congregation that a few years later reported 185 members. The best mergers tend to be when three congregations come together to create a new congregation that constructs a new building at a new site under a new name with the strong leadership of a new minister.

While painful, perhaps the easiest and certainly one of the most widely followed alternatives is to dissolve. When that combination of kinship ties, denominational loyalties, nationality heritage, and geographical convenience no longer produces the necessary replacement members, the decision often is between change and institutional death. An average of fifty to sixty congregations in American Protestantism choose to dissolve every week compared to perhaps five to ten that are able and willing to redefine their role.

A fifth alternative is to do nothing and passively watch as the congregation grows older and smaller. The decision is to postpone making a decision.

A sixth alternative, and the favorite of many, is to attempt to recreate 1924 or 1954. This choice was illustrated by this conversation in early 1990.

"For at least eighty years this was the only Norwegian Lutheran parish in this end of the county," reflected the thirty-three-year-old pastor of the 235-member congregation in a small midwestern community. "Then with the merger of 1960 this became one of four congregations affiliated with the American Lutheran Church, all of whom serve the same general area. Now, with the merger that created the new Evangelical Lutheran Church in America, we are now one of nine parishes of the same denomination in this general community. It seems to me we have to talk about either carving out a new role for ourselves or perhaps merging with another nearby Lutheran congregation."

"I'm afraid you're right, Pastor," agreed a seventy-four-year-old member in a sorrowful voice. "The boats aren't coming over from the old country anymore. But you know, Pastor, if the unrest that is present in Latvia, Lithuania, and Estonia spreads to Scandinavia, maybe we'll get a whole new wave of Norwegians coming to this country."

Relatively few congregations, however, succeed in their effort to recreate yesterday. This often is the next-to-last chapter in that congregation's history. If that effort fails, the next chapter usually is either merger or dissolution.

What Is Our Niche?

A seventh alternative, which was introduced back in chapter 4, usually requires a four-part strategy which consists of (a) changing the basic focus of ministry, (b) shifting from a geographical to a non-geographical definition of role and/or from a historic nationality, language, racial, or ethnic heritage, (c) identifying the religious needs of people that are not being met by other churches in that area and matching these needs against the resources of that congregation in determining the priorities in program planning, and (d) building a coalition of leaders that includes the pastor and four or five creative and energetic lay volunteers who will accept the responsibility for proposing and implementing a new course of action.

Occasionally a congregation can build a new future as a geographical parish, but this is so rare that it seldom can be used as a model by others.

Far more common is the shift to a non-geographical definition of a new niche or distinctive role. The more limited the resources of the congregation, the more likely it will be to choose a distinctive niche rather than seek to become a "full service congregation" offering the full range of programming necessary to meet the religious needs of a diverse collection of people.

What Are the Possibilities?

This concept of a specialized niche is illustrated by recent trends in American television. For nearly three decades television was dominated by the three networks, each of which sought to serve the entire American population, plus public television. The next chapter brought cable. By late 1990 the 56 million homes with cable had access to a huge array of specialized channels. One company carved out a distinctive niche with sports, several others with music, another with cowboy music and movies, two with news, a couple with business, one for lawyers, a couple with comedy, and two more with courtroom drama. By late 1990 most cable television channels represented specialized niches and only a few companies aimed for a broad heterogeneous audience. A parallel trend can be seen among the churches, especially in urban areas. A few examples will illustrate this concept of a specialized niche.

1. One of the most redemptive is that specialized ministry with the recently widowed by widowed members. Very, very few congregations provide an effective ministry with recently widowed women under forty-five years of age or with widowed men. In the average week nearly 20,000 marriages are terminated by the death of one spouse. One result is that the American population now includes 11 million widowed women and 2 million widowed men. This can be a highly redemptive and

unique ministry for the congregation that includes a large number of widows and widowers.

2. A radically different niche is the ministry built around music and young children. The special niche that can draw people from a huge radius is the program that enables young children to express their creativity and to communicate through music, especially instrumental music. This requires a leader with special training in that field.

3. A growing number of churches have found a special niche in a ministry with blended families consisting of several couples, each with one or more children from a previous marriage.

4. A few churches have built a new future with a ministry with hurting women. While this often means a high turnover in membership, it can be a remarkably redemptive ministry.

5. Several smaller congregations have built a unique niche by challenging people, especially mature adults, to be engaged in ministry with others. This may include the annual work camp mission trip to another country or a crew that helps construct the first meetinghouse for a new congregation or a partnership with a nearby nursing home or children's home. A parallel, and compatible, niche is a similar emphasis designed to reach young adults born after 1968. This can create an interesting mixture of people from different generations working together on outreach ministries.

6. A rapidly growing number of congregations have carved out a new niche, often following the arrival of a pastor in his or her second marriage, in building a ministry with couples who are in their second or subsequent marriage.

7. One of the more rapidly growing specialized ministries is with gays and lesbians, and/or parents of gays and lesbians, who feel rejected by the traditional churches.

8. One of the more popular niches is to become a learning center where seekers, inquirers, searchers, and pilgrims come to learn more about the Christian faith. Many expressions of this concept exist, but most require excellent teachers, plus a far above average level of openness to new Christians. This is easier for new missions to implement than for long-established churches.

9. One of the great unmet needs is to provide a warm and

supportive church home for the rapidly growing number of single parent families.

10. A growing number of congregations have responded to the increasing number of parents who seek a small, high quality, and avowedly Christian day school for their children. This may, however, turn out to be more than a niche to enable that congregation to remain on a plateau in size. It can become the central component of a dynamic strategy for numerical growth. This is most likely to happen if the goal is to reach and serve upwardly mobile working class families, both black and white, who are driven by the dream of a better life for their children.

11. Several dozen congregations, most of them averaging fewer than a hundred people at worship, have defined a distinctive role with the central organizing principle of feeding the hungry, educating the handicapped child, sheltering the homeless, caring for the unwed mother and her child, or a similar combined social action-community outreach focus.

12. While it is not the easiest choice to implement, a growing number of congregations have decided to become intentionally bilingual churches that bring together both first and second generation immigrant families with third, fourth, and fifth generation Anglo-Americans.

Is your congregation ready to think about a new role or a special niche in ministry?

Could this be a relevant and creative beginning point for the deliberations of the long-range planning committee in your church? If so, these three questions belong near the top of the agenda.

1. In previous decades were (a) kinship ties and/or (b) denominational loyalties and/or (c) a nationality, language, racial, or ethnic heritage and/or (d) geographical convenience influential factors in determining who united with this parish?

2. If yes, how attractive are those forces in attracting new generations of members for today and tomorrow?

3. How many of your members agree the time has come to redefine the role of this congregation and to carve out a new and distinctive niche in terms of outreach and ministry? If that list includes three to five of your most widely respected and influential members, go to it! That is all you need.

CHAPTER EIGHT

What Does It Cost to Go to Church?

"SEVEN DOLLARS FOR A TWO-HOUR MOVIE?" EXCLAIMED HARRY Perkins in dismay when he reached the ticket window at a downtown motion picture theater. "Back home I can go to the movies for two dollars in the afternoon and three-fifty in the evening. I've never paid seven dollars for a movie in my whole life!"

"When I found out the airline wanted $450 for a round-trip ticket to fly from Chicago to Minneapolis and back, I decided to drive," explained Ruth Javier. "That figures out to 56 cents a mile. I can drive it for less than that and not have to worry about getting out to the airport and back."

Many people find it easy and useful to compare costs for a movie or for traveling from one city to another, but few make the same effort to calculate what it costs to go to church. For some leaders that is a repugnant idea; they believe the focus should be on stewardship, not costs. It may be useful, however, for your long-range planning committee to look at the costs of going to your church.

A far more widely used, but less valuable, approach is to examine per capita giving. This procedure usually means dividing the grand total of all tithes and contributions by the membership. In 1990 this procedure produced averages that ranged from $200 per confirmed member in thousands of churches to over $1,000 per member in several denominations. Most denominations reported per confirmed member averages between $200 and $700. That is such a broad range as to be of little value. One reason, of course, is the huge variations in the definition of "member."

A better method is to use the average attendance at worship, rather than membership, as the divisor. In 1990 most churches averaged out to between $600 and $1,000 using this method. In other words, total contributions were the equivalent of $700 to $800 times the average attendance at worship. Thus the church averaging 200 at worship could expect $140,000 to $160,000 in contributions in 1990. (For 1993 those averages probably will be closer to $800 to $1,000 times the average worship attendance.) Some remarkably thrifty congregations with no indebtedness or substantial capital improvements were able to pay all their bills in 1990 with contributions that totaled $350 to $500 times the worship attendance. At the other end of that long spectrum scores of large churches with extensive weekday programming and/or large expenditures for capital improvements and/or very large allocations for missions needed to receive $1,500 to $3,000 times their average worship attendance in order to meet all their obligations that year.

Measuring Unit Costs

A third, and less frequently used, system that can be useful for comparisons is to assume that (a) all receipts come via the offering plate, (b) all expenditures will be made out of those offerings, and (c) everyone in attendance should and will contribute an equal amount each time he or she is present for worship. No more than one congregation in 100,000 will meet all three of those criteria, but that model can be used to illustrate the distribution of costs. For discussion purposes, let us use a congregation that averages 150 people at worship, pays all bills out of members' contributions, has no other income, and in 1991 operated with a budget of $120,000.

When $120,000 is divided by that average attendance of 150, that means $800 per year per attender. When that $800 is divided by 52 weeks, that averages out to $15.38. That means that the husband-wife couple who come to church with one child should put $46.14 in the offering plate every time the three of them participate in that Sunday worship service. That reflects the average cost per attender per Sunday of $15.38.

Where Does It Go?

Let us next assume this congregation has to budget $6,000 annually for the maintenance of this seventy-four-year-old building plus another $1,000 monthly to meet the principal and interest payments on the mortgage resulting from the renovation of the building that was completed four years ago. (Or this $12,000 annual debt service payment could be for the purchase of the house next door that was razed in order to expand the parking lot or from a modest addition completed a few years ago.)

That $18,000 total is equal to 15 percent of that $120,000 budget. That is a typical percentage. In some congregations maintenance of the meeting place and mortgage payments may be as high as 25 percent or as low as 5 percent, but 15 percent is typical. That means $2.31 of that $15.38 average weekly contribution goes for this purpose. (If that is the year of a major capital funds campaign to raise money for a new building program, the combined total of capital fund contributions, maintenance of the meeting place, and mortgage payments may account for more than one-half of total receipts for that one year.)

If this is an average congregation, 16 percent of all member giving is allocated to benevolences, missions, and denominational causes. (In larger congregations this proportion often ranges between 20 and 35 percent, but 16 percent is a common figure for churches averaging 150 to 300 at worship.) This means 16 percent of that $15.38 or $2.46 goes for benevolences and missions.

The proportion of the total member giving allocated to staff salaries and benefits, including housing, ranges from 70 percent in thousands of small churches that have a full-time resident pastor down to 25 or 30 percent in the very large congregations with a highly productive staff and a powerful tradition of generous support for missions. The typical congregation averaging 400 to 500 at worship may allocate 15 percent for maintenance of the meeting place and debt service, 25 to 30 percent for benevolences, 15 to 20 percent for program, and 35 to 45 percent for staff salaries and benefits, including housing.

The congregation averaging 150 at worship may provide the pastor with a total compensation package of $45,000 (cash salary, housing, utilities, health insurance, pension, continuing education, travel or car allowance, and other benefits). That comes out to 37.5 percent of that $120,000 or $5.77 for each worshiper each Sunday.

This same congregation may allocate another $15,000 for cash salary and benefits (social security, pension) for the compensation of a part-time church secretary, a part-time choir director, and a part-time custodian. That is an additional 12.5 percent of that $120,000 budget and means one-half of that total is allocated for staff salaries and benefits, including housing costs.

At this point we add building maintenance and debt service (15 percent) to benevolences (16 percent) and staff costs (50 percent) and discover we have 19 percent left. It turns out that 19 percent of $120,000 comes out to $22,800.

That $22,800, or $2.92 per attender per Sunday, may be used to pay for the Sunday school literature, utilities, bulletins for worship, insurance, printing and mailing the monthly newsletter, postage, stationery, a couple of guest preachers every year, tuition for continuing education experience for volunteers, newspaper advertising, candles, materials for the annual stewardship program, a direct mail campaign to invite the unchurched to come here, music and supplies for the choir, a paid adult to staff the nursery on Sunday mornings, janitorial supplies, committee expenses, the costs of the Vacation Bible School held every summer, tuning the piano, the service contracts on the office equipment, and other program expenses. In smaller congregations or in churches with only a modest weekday program, that proportion may be in the 10 to 15 percent range. It also should be noted again that in the first year of a big capital funds campaign, total member contributions may average out to $35 to $50 per week per worshiper with one-half to three-quarters of that grand total going into that capital funds campaign, only 15 to 20 percent being allocated to staff compensation, perhaps as little as 10 percent for benevolences, and another 5 to 10 percent for program. That is a one-year phenomenon, however, not a typical pattern!

Another Potential Beginning Point

If the primary reason for creating this long-range planning committee is a financial squeeze, this can be a useful beginning point. In other churches this procedure represents the beginning point for the preparation of next year's budget. Instead of being locked into the past by beginning with the figures for last year's receipts and expenditures, the budget committee begins by discussing priorities and proportions. What percentage of our anticipated receipts must we allocate to our obligations for paying off the mortgage and for the anticipated maintenance of our real estate? This often is the easiest set of financial projections to calculate.

Next, what proportion of our total receipts, including special appeals and designated second-mile giving, do we plan to allocate to benevolences and missions? What is our target for that?

Third, what proportion must we allocate for staff salaries and benefits including housing? As was pointed out earlier, the basic generalization is the larger the size of the congregation, the larger the proportion for benevolences. Occasionally, however, the congregation that has been on a plateau in size for years and is now committed to moving up off that plateau[1] may boost the proportion for staff costs in order to employ a specialist in new member enlistment, perhaps on a part-time basis. Since 100 percent is a fixed beginning point, this means a reduction in the proportion allocated to program or benevolences or real estate. That can be tempered by increasing the size of the pie. Thus the congregation averaging 180 at worship may increase the *amount* for staff compensation from $70,000 to $90,000 by increasing the total budget by $25,000. This would result in a reduction in the *percentages* for other budget categories, but still allow for a modest increase in the actual dollar figures for those other budget items.

Other church growth strategies will require an increase in both the dollars and percentages allocated to program—perhaps from 12 percent to 20 or 25 percent.

After a tentative percentage figure has been arrived at for real estate, benevolences, and staff compensation, the next step is to agree on a proportion for program. This may require some compromises on those other percentages. When agreement has been reached, these percentages are forwarded to the governing board for review and approval. The next stage is to translate the percentages into dollar figures. In some churches this is done before the members are asked to make financial commitments for the coming year. In others these percentages are used to allocate the anticipated receipts for the new fiscal year. In a growing number of churches the stewardship committee completes its program before any budget is presented for next year. One reason for that is to encourage people to make their financial commitment in response to how God has blessed them, not to underwrite a budget.[2]

Up or Down?

"If the size of congregations in American Protestantism is increasing and if the number of megachurches has quintupled since 1950, these unit costs should be going down, shouldn't they? Churches should benefit from the economy of scale just like automobile manufacturers, shouldn't they?"

The answer is no. Churches should be compared to municipal governments, hospitals, schools, legal firms, and other agencies providing person-centered services. It is true that economies of scale can be achieved in many segments of the economy such as grocery stores, where some of the labor costs were shifted from the retailer to the customer in the 1930–60 era, but in others unit costs go up as size goes up. Five examples of higher unit costs as size goes up are municipal government, hospitals, schools, legal firms, and churches. Why?

Among the many reasons are (1) the increase in the number and range of services offered, (2) the rise in the level of quality, (3) the need for more experienced and highly skilled specialists, and they cost more than less experienced generalists, (4) higher administrative costs, and (5) higher costs for real estate.

The consumer price index quintupled in the period from 1953 to 1991, from 80 to over 400 (1967=100). The average unit costs of operating the average Protestant church in the United States, however, increased somewhere between eight and twelve times during those thirty-eight years. Thus the person born in 1923 who was on the finance committee of a Protestant church back in 1953 may recall, "I can remember when we figured we needed a dollar and a half from every person in church every Sunday to pay our bills. Now you're telling me we need fifteen dollars?"

A common answer to that question is yes. In many rural churches the unit costs have jumped from fifty cents in 1953 to eight dollars in 1991. In the typical suburban congregation the unit costs in 1991 were nine to fifteen times the figure for 1953.

Per Capita Personal Income USA	
1930	$ 613
1940	507
1950	1,504
1953	1,806
1960	2,265
1970	4,056
1980	9,916
1987	15,495
1990 (Est.)	17,900

For comparison purposes per capita personal income in the United States increased approximately tenfold from 1953 to 1991. In those congregations where the average expenditures per attender per Sunday have climbed from $1.50 in 1953 to $15.00 in 1990 or 1991, the cost of going to church has increased at the same pace as the rise in per capita personal income. In literally thousands of small rural churches, however, those unit costs have climbed from forty or fifty or sixty cents to a dollar per worshiper per Sunday in 1953 to eight to twenty dollars in 1991. Those changes help explain why so many small congregations feel they no longer can afford a full-time seminary trained and experienced resident pastor. Their costs have increased far more rapidly than their receipts.

An examination of unit costs in slightly over three thousand congregations reveals five major variables. The most significant, the most subjective, and the most difficult to agree on is the productivity of the paid staff. If five is the number assigned to symbolize the level of productivity of the average full-time Protestant staff person, a significant number fall in the two to four bracket, a smaller group ranges between seven and fifteen, and a tiny handful earn a grade for their productivity of twenty to thirty. Thus the congregation with a highly productive staff will have lower unit costs than one that receives an average to below average level of productivity from the paid staff.

A second variable is the type of ministry that occupies a considerable proportion of staff time and energy. Three of the high cost ministries are youth groups, younger, never-married adult programming, and Christian day schools. At the other end of the scale are those congregations that emphasize the role of lay-led and lay-owned organizations such as the women's organization, the Sunday school, and the men's fellowship. These tend to be very low cost ministries.

A third variable is location. Unit costs are higher in San Diego than in Peoria, higher in New York City than in Augusta, Georgia, and higher in Boston than in Garden City, Kansas. One reason, of course, is the cost of housing for paid staff.

A fourth variable is the salary scale. While many, many exceptions exist, churches that are experiencing numerical decline often pay a higher level of compensation to staff than is offered the staff in congregations experiencing rapid numerical growth. This should come as no surprise to students of religious organizations or to those who have examined the differences between a new movement and the long-established organization committed to meeting the needs of its own constituency. This may surprise some dyed-in-the-wool capitalists, however.

That combination of higher expenditures and shrinking numbers naturally produces rising unit costs.

A fifth variable is the real estate. Many congregations meet in ancient, functionally obsolete, and deteriorating high cost buildings. Others meet in completely paid for, well-designed, and thrifty buildings. That difference can amount to two to three dollars per week per worshiper.

Does your congregation fall in the high cost end of this spectrum or the low cost end? That difference may be as much as fifteen or twenty dollars per Sunday per attender! If you are in a high cost congregation, that could be a good beginning point for a special ad hoc study committee.

CHAPTER NINE

Tradition or Market?

"I CAN'T UNDERSTAND WHY YOU'RE SUGGESTING THREE SERVICES on Christmas Eve when we never fill the church for either of the two we now have," protested Ray Bolton. "Last year we could have accommodated another twenty people at the seven o'clock service and at least a hundred more at the eleven o'clock Communion Service."

"Not only that, but there are a lot of members who wish we could go back to just one service on Christmas Eve," added Lillian Johnson. "They liked it better when the whole church came together at one time. Now they complain they don't see a lot of their old friends who come to church at the other hour."

"You may not believe this," reported Sam Welch to the other members of this special committee that had been appointed to design the schedule and plan the Christmas Eve services for this coming December, "but I just got back from a visit with my brother and his wife up in Minnesota. They're both serving on the committee responsible for planning their Christmas Eve program, and they are projecting *six different* services for this December. The first is a four o'clock Christmas party for Jesus designed for very young children who may not be interested in discussions about the virgin birth, but who are old enough to know what a birthday party is. The five-thirty service is being planned for families with five-, six-, and seven-year-old children. The seven o'clock service is for families of all ages with lots of Christmas carols. The eight-thirty service will be built around the music of the high school choir. The ten o'clock service will feature the church orchestra, and at eleven-thirty they are planning a silent Communion Service. That's six different services designed for six different audiences!"

"That would never work here," observed Ray Bolton sourly. "Our people like tradition and our tradition here is two services on Christmas Eve. That's the way it's been ever since our current pastor came nine years ago, and that's the way it'll be this year if I have anything to say about it. Those who have children who need to go to bed early or want to go home and open their presents on Christmas Eve come to the early service. Those who want to stay up late come to the Communion Service. Why in the world any church would offer six services is beyond me unless they have a severe shortage of space or a workaholic pastor. We don't have either one, so I don't think your brother's church experience is relevant here, Sam."

"I think it is relevant," protested Sam, "and I'll tell you why. That church is trying to reach younger generations of people, and one way they do it is to offer people a broad range of choices. Another is they understand that in many parts of the country Christmas Eve can be the biggest and most attractive re-entry point for adults under forty who dropped out of church ten or twenty years ago. My brother's church is taking advantage of that and it's working! That church is growing younger and larger while our congregation is growing older and smaller."

★ ★ ★

This conversation illustrates several issues that should be on the agenda of the long-range planning committee of your church. Perhaps the least significant is what you plan to do on Christmas Eve. For many long-established congregations the central point illustrated by this conversation is the fact that for many people who dropped out of church several years ago, Christmas Eve can be the number-one re-entry point.

The big question for your long-range planning committee is illustrated by the contrast between these two viewpoints. Ray Bolton insists tradition should rule. By contrast, Sam Welch argues the churches should be responsive to the needs of the people in today's world. Parallel discussions about the conflict between tradition and contemporary reality have been going on for decades in higher education, marketing, government, military organizations, the public schools, labor unions, lodges, hospitals, veterans' organizations, and publishing. This is not a new debate.

The churches, like most long-established institutions, tend to be driven by the weight of tradition. One example of this is the Roman Catholic Church. A second is the congregation that rejects a proposal to relocate to a larger, more accessible, and more highly visible site in order to reach new generations of people, in favor of remaining at the old sacred site, even though that almost certainly means growing older and smaller.

Most Protestant churches in North America are heavily influenced by tradition, custom, past precedents, history, and their own institutional culture. Unless a new and powerful force is introduced into the equation, the standard expectation is tomorrow will resemble today. The beginning point for preparing next year's budget is this year's budget. The comparison base for evaluating the new pastor is the personality, performance, and gifts of the previous minister. The criterion for deciding on the number of bulletins to be reproduced for this next Sunday's worship service is the number used last Sunday, perhaps with a look at the number required for the equivalent Sunday last year. The evaluation of the size of the current youth group will be a comparison with last year's numbers. The beginning point for a recommendation for the minister's compensation for next year will be this year's compensation. The assignment of rooms to Sunday school classes will begin with past usage.

The history of American Protestantism reveals thousands of occasions when the battle over tradition produced remarkably divisive internal conflicts. The list of these divisive issues includes the language to be used in corporate worship, barring lodge members from membership, the age of baptism, indoor plumbing, the ownership of an automobile by the pastor, slavery, permitting men to wear a necktie to worship, the authority of the Pope over a Catholic president, the remarriage of divorced people, the singing of hymns rather than only the Psalms, the wearing of wedding rings, showing motion pictures in the church, dancing in the church, designated giving, the central pulpit versus the divided chancel, the wearing of a robe by the pastor, racial integration, facial hair on men, videotaping the worship service, using graded materials in the Sunday school, introducing instrumental music, installing a telephone in the church building ("This means our pastor no longer will make home calls."), permitting women to serve on the governing board, granting the pastor a housing allowance rather than requiring residence in a church-owned parsonage or manse, paying someone to direct the choir, replacing that ancient piano with an electronic keyboard, hiring someone rather than depending solely on volunteers to staff the nursery, the ordination of women, the use of buttons rather than a hook and eye on garments, bishops, providing off-street parking, replacing the piano with an organ, using electricity to illuminate the inside of the church, evolution, the use of tobacco by parishioners, missions, Sabbath observance, bobbed hair, robing the choir, and baptizing children under age twelve.

Even more significant is how tradition can reinforce the strong member orientation of these churches. The top priority on the pastor's time is assumed to be the care of today's members. The Sunday morning schedule is determined by the preferences of the members in general and the volunteer leaders in particular. The Sunday morning worship experience is designed to meet the needs of believers in general and today's members in particular. The ministries with teenagers usually are designed and scheduled with the hope of serving the children of today's members.

In some congregations this strong member orientation prohibits the pastor from officiating at a wedding in which neither party is a member or from conducting the funeral service for a nonmember. In other congregations this strong member orientation often means that special events, such as the Christmas Eve services or that Thanksgiving morning service or Saturday evening worship, are designed, scheduled, and publicized on the assumption these are for the benefit of members. The total ministry of music, the choices of hymns, and the liturgy are chosen to please today's members.

In some congregations this powerful member orientation is altered by the influence of outside factors that shape the life and ministry of these churches. Among the most highly visible examples are theological seminaries, building codes and zoning ordinances, television, continuing education events for both the laity and the clergy, the denominational committee that created a new hymnal, the lectionary, denominational mergers, the system for ministerial placement, and various denominationally initiated priorities.

The most highly visible consequence of this strong member orientation is that it facilitates the process of growing older and smaller. The stronger the pressures of tradition and the greater the member orientation, the more likely that congregation will shrink in numbers as the members grow older.

This powerful member orientation often shows up early in the discussions of the long-range planning committee when someone suggests, "I believe the first thing we should do is survey our members to see what they want." (See chapter 2.) That usually produces wishes to re-create yesterday.

If the pressures to conduct a survey are irresistible, a wiser choice would be to visit and interview all of last year's one-time visitors who subsequently decided to join another church in this community. An alternative would be to visit adults who do not attend any church and seek to discover what might interest them. Or a third survey could be of members who have left your congregation to attend another church in this community.

A Useful Beginning Point

Rather than plunge into that extremely complicated process of taking and interpreting surveys, the long-range planning committee may be well advised to choose another beginning point. Frequently this can be a provocative beginning point for these deliberations. Should we seek to identify, understand, and affirm all the many traditions that have shaped this congregation over the years and to seek to perpetuate those traditions? Or should we seek to be open to the power of the Holy Spirit to redefine the role of this congregation in this place in this day and to carve out a new niche for this parish?

That Market-Driven Minority

A small, but growing, minority of Protestant congregations have examined this pair of alternatives and chosen the second. Many of these are new congregations. Others chose this alternative after the arrival of a new pastor. In both cases most are driven by a desire to reach, attract, and serve new generations of youth and adults. In a few extreme examples, the Sunday morning worship experience is designed for seekers, persons on a religious pilgrimage, skeptics, inquirers, first-time visitors, and searchers. The worship service designed for the committed Christians is scheduled for another time during the week.

The basic distinction between these two approaches to the world was described in an award-winning book, *Innovation in Marketing*, by Theodore Levitt.[1] This book, which was written for a business, not a church audience, lifts up the difference between focusing on the needs of the seller rather than on the needs of the buyer. Levitt urges the reader to concentrate on the needs of the people, rather than on the needs of the institution. Literally scores of books and influential articles have been published during the past three decades by other authors who emphasize this same point. This perspective calls for focusing on the needs of the consumer of the services or program, not on the producer's needs. This perspective also is often a part of the culture of today's megachurches.

This is a difficult expectation to place on the tradition-bound church which finds it easier to attempt to perpetuate yesterday than to create a new tomorrow. If that is true for your congregation, that may call for the members of your long-range planning committee to see themselves as interventionists for change, not as perpetuators of the status quo. This often places a premium on seeking members for that committee who are highly competent in initiating planned change from within an organization rather than on assembling a representative cross section of members. (See chapter 2.)

Perhaps the most common and highly visible example of this distinction between tradition-bound and market-driven can be found in the advertisements on the church page of the Friday or Saturday newspapers. In most newspapers the vast majority of these ads resemble the "tombstone" notice run by a stockbroker announcing a new bond issue or the sale of new stock in a company. This satisfies certain legal requirements. The parallel is the ad run by a church that announces the name and address of a particular congregation plus the Sunday schedule and the names of the staff. It may include a line drawing of the building plus the text and title for Sunday's sermon. That satisfies those who contend, "We should advertise our church in the newspaper."

Once in awhile, however, that same page will carry a church ad that is addressed to the needs of the reader. Relatively few of the words in these ads relate to the publisher. Most of the words are directed to the religious pilgrimage and needs of the reader.

A second example of this market-driven approach surfaced back in the 1960s when dozens of congregations made the changes necessary to attract and welcome the so-called "Jesus People." Among the most common of these changes was a willingness to relax the dress code, to expand the Sunday school, to accept different music, to double or triple the number of worshipers, to enlarge the teaching ministry, and to add new staff members to serve the increased numbers.

A third example is in those denominations willing to create new congregations to reach and serve the wave of immigrants from Central and South America and the Pacific Rim. This usually required postponing that dream of integrating all immigrants into Anglo churches, changes in the requirements for ministerial standing, and more multilingual publications.

A fourth example is in new church development directed at younger generations of the population. This usually has meant abandoning the traditional approaches to ministerial training, ordination, and placement; accepting and utilizing new approaches to new member enlistment; creating a different format for corporate worship; dropping the old pattern of beginning small in the hope of growing larger, in favor of beginning large; offering very modest or no financial subsidies; emphasizing a far greater sensitivity to the needs of people and less dependence on denominational or institutional loyalties; affirming a greater recognition of the power of excellent preaching and top quality oral communication; and offering prospective members meaningful choices.[2]

Two Questions for Your Committee

Two general questions should be addressed by your long-range planning committee if you choose this as your beginning point for that group's deliberations.

First, what is contemporary reality? Are we in fact a tradition-bound church? Or are decisions here made with an openness to new ideas and a desire to identify, reach, and serve new generations of people who will not find our traditions sufficient reason for coming here?

To be more precise, what does your advertisement in the local newspaper suggest? What does your staffing configuration indicate are your priorities? What does your Sunday morning schedule suggest? The system for financing your church? The openness to organizing new classes and groups? The responses to proposals to change the schedule? To expand the weekday program? To what degree does your real estate, your denominational affiliation, and your tradition influence today's policies, priorities, and schedules?

Another means of testing reality is to spend several hours or longer visiting at least three or four rapidly growing congregations that are attracting large numbers of people born after 1955. Are they market-driven? How do your policies and practices compare with theirs?

The second general question is a simple one to articulate, but it may be painful to discuss. Do we want to give the higher priority to reinforcing and perpetuating tradition? Or will the higher priority be placed on identifying and responding to the religious needs of new generations of adults?

In his book Theodore Levitt distinguishes between "pushing your product" and responding to the needs of people.

Do you expect new people to come to your church to fill your empty pews, to help support your budget, to contribute to those annual payments on the mortgage, to staff your Sunday school, and to accept without question your priorities, policies, traditions, and schedules? Or are your leaders willing to change the shape of the vessel that carries the Good News that Jesus Christ is Lord and Savior?

CHAPTER TEN

No Surprises!

"THE ONE POINT ON WHICH I HOPE WE ALL CAN AGREE," URGED Joe Hannah, a member of the newly formed futures committee at Calvary Church, "is that what is said in this room stays in this room. When we're done, we'll make a full report at a congregational meeting, but let's not feed the grapevine a lot of rumors, tentative proposals, and half-baked ideas."

"I can't buy that!" exclaimed Audrey Jones. "I believe we must make periodic progress reports to the congregation on our deliberations. Maybe we could have a progress report column in our monthly parish newsletter?"

"I am in complete disagreement with you, Joe," added Jason Barkley, the youngest member of the committee. "This is a free country and that includes free speech. I want everyone here to understand that I will feel completely free to discuss any phase of our planning with anyone of my choice. In fact, I believe that would be good if we all did that. That not only will help keep our people informed about what we're considering, that also will be a way of feeding the ideas and concerns of our members into our discussions. I think I understand the possible disruption the grapevine can create, but I believe keeping secrets in the churches creates far more serious risks!"

"I'm not suggesting that everything we say or do be a deep secret," protested Joe. "All I'm saying is we should be careful to avoid premature disclosures of what we're considering. We are certain to examine and discuss alternative courses of action that subsequently are rejected. Why encourage people to get all worked up over something that we may never recommend?"

"This is an important question," interjected Bobbie Brancato, "but it seems to me the answer is obvious. With seven of us on this committee, I think it is completely unrealistic to guarantee there will be no leaks. Since we can't guarantee complete secrecy, let's adopt a policy now that declares all our meetings are open to any member who wants to come and listen to our discussions. I also believe we should adopt Audrey's suggestion to publish a progress report in our monthly parish newsletter."

What Are Your Assumptions?

This discussion raises a critical policy question for the long-range planning committee. One way to state it is secrecy versus open meetings. A better way may be to examine the assumptions on which the committee operates. Five merit consideration here.

The first, and one of the safest, is from that day the decision was made to create a long-range planning committee, the process of building support or opposition has been underway. One of the obvious steps in this process is the choice of criteria to be used in selecting the members of the committee. Another is the choice of the person to chair it. A third is in the content of the leaks, progress reports, and recommendations that come out of the committee.

If that assumption is valid, one of the questions that should be on the agenda at every meeting is, How do we build support for our eventual recommendations? Should we work at building early support for our eventual recommendations? Or should we hope and pray support will be offered when we need it, but do nothing ourselves to mobilize it?

A second assumption is that most adults tend to respond negatively when surprised. Most normal people need time to talk themselves into supporting a new idea. Therefore periodic progress reports from the long-range planning committee can minimize the surprises encountered by members when the final report is released.

An excellent example of this came from a long-range planning committee that eventually recommended employing a full-time professional to create and oversee a weekday Early Childhood Development Center in that parish. This news came to the congregation in ten stages.

The first progress report recommended a high priority be given to reaching and serving parents of young children.

A second report suggested this be the number-one priority in program expansion.

A third report summarized the changes in the building that the city building inspector would require for weekday programming with children.

A fourth report conveyed the estimated costs made by a local contractor of those improvements to the real estate.

A fifth report stated one adult Sunday school class had agreed to pay one-half the costs of those changes.

A sixth report thanked the women's organization for agreeing to pay the other half of those remodeling costs.

A seventh report outlined the preliminary plans for this weekday program.

An eighth report described the proposed staff and the anticipated operating costs for this program.

A ninth report estimated receipts from user fees and the amount that parish would have to contribute beyond the income from fees.

A final report summarized all the above and also included a request for permission to begin recruiting a director if the report was approved.

This entire process required seven months, and the recommendations in that final report were unanimously approved at a congregational meeting.

This committee recognized and accepted the responsibility for building support for its recommendations many months before that congregational meeting was held.

A third assumption, which is more difficult for some people to accept, is that the interaction between the members of the committee and people from the congregation actually may stimulate creative thinking and improve the quality of the final recommendations.

A fourth assumption, which some readers will insist should head this list, relates to the concept of "ownership" and eventual implementation of the recommendations. The safe assumption is, "My idea is more attractive to me than is your idea."

If the recommendations from this planning committee will require (a) the time and energy of volunteers and/or (b) financial contributions from people other than those on the committee and/or (c) approval at a congregational meeting and/or (d) changes in schedules, room use, traditions, budgets, staff, or other priorities and/or (e) changes in the real estate, prudence suggests that it may be wise to broaden the base of support long before the final report is issued.

Finally, in most churches a safe assumption is that recommendations for substantial changes will not be implemented without the active and unreserved support of the pastor or senior minister. Any pastor who has earned the title of "leader" should be able to veto any proposal for change. The larger the size of the congregation, the more likely that will be a valid assumption.

Therefore, a critical component of building that support base is winning the approval of the pastor. In the vast majority of churches this is not a significant concern since the pastor usually accepts an active role in that planning process. One exception is the pastor who prefers a passive or non-directive role. A second is when a new minister arrives a month or two or three before the long-range planning committee issues its report. In either case it is worth the time and effort required to win active support from the pastor before any final set of recommendations is issued.

What is the policy of your long-range planning committee on this question of secrecy versus regular progress reports? What are the assumptions on which that policy is based? Is that policy, and its implications, consistent with building support for the committee's recommendation? What is the role of your pastor in this?

CHAPTER ELEVEN

To Study or to Act?

"ALTHOUGH I NEVER REALLY EXPECTED THIS TO HAPPEN, I AM delighted that we were able to arrive at unanimous support for this set of recommendations," commented Bert Jackson, who had chaired the long-range planning committee at Bethany Church for the past ten months. "This is our fourteenth meeting, and six months ago I wondered if we could muster a majority vote for a motion to disband this committee. I guess this proves what patience, prayer, goodwill, trust, persistence, and study can do. I'm proud of you all, and I'm proud of what we have agreed on as a six-point strategy for Bethany. We now need a motion to have this set of recommendations typed, printed, and sent to the church council. That will be our last official action, and then we can disband this committee. Our assignment will have been completed."

"Wait a minute!" exclaimed Ronnie Brown. "We can't just turn our report over to the council and disband. We need to continue to meet and to function until we're sure all six of these recommendations are being implemented."

"I don't think you understand our assignment," explained Bert gently. "Our charge was to design a comprehensive action plan for Bethany Church for the next five years. We've done that. We're a study committee, not an action committee. Our assignment was to come up with a plan. It is now up to the church council to implement that plan."

"You're a lot more optimistic than I am if you think the church council will carry out these recommendations," grumbled Ronnie. "The basic reason we needed an action plan is that the church council here always has been a maintenance operation. It has never been an initiating group. I know. I was on it for six years. All we ever did was meet, talk, listen to reports, approve some committee's proposal, adopt a schedule for the year, recommend approval of the budget prepared by the finance committee, and complain about the lack of loyalty of so many of our members. If you think this church council will take the initiative in implementing our recommendations, there's a bridge in Brooklyn I would like to sell you. Either we do it or it won't get done and we will have wasted ten months of hard work!"

As has been emphasized repeatedly in earlier pages, most long-range planning committees are faced with several pivotal decisions. One is the criteria for selecting the members. A second is to make that choice between creating a grand design or concentrating on a single subject. A third is the choice of a planning model. A fourth is in deciding what data should be gathered. A fifth is the choice of a beginning point for mapping out that road into the future. A sixth is that choice between operating in secrecy versus regular and full disclosure. A seventh is the choice between serving as an ad hoc study committee that submits a series of recommendations or combining that assignment with the role of an ad hoc action committee.

Five Choices

The late Ohio State football coach Woody Hayes once was asked, "Coach Hayes, why do you place so much emphasis on the run and so little on the forward pass?" According to legend, Hayes replied, "When your quarterback throws a forward pass, only four things can happen, and three of them are bad."

What can happen to this carefully prepared set of recommendations about to be reported by Bert Jackson's long-range planning committee at Bethany Church?

The answer is five—and three of them are bad. A common choice is to submit a printed report to the governing board that accepts it, adopts by a unanimous vote a resolution of gratitude to those faithful members who prepared the report, and files it. That is the end of that story.

A second alternative is for the governing board to sort out the recommendations and refer two to the trustees, three to the Christian education committee, one to the women's organization, two to the finance committee, one to the missions committee, one to the ushers, four to the membership committee, two to the evangelism committee (which had its most recent meeting nineteen months ago), and the rest to the minister. That completes the responsibilities of both the long-range planning committee and the governing board. Eventually three of the recommendations are implemented—one by the trustees because it turned into an emergency, one by the women's organization because that is the one group in most congregations that is highly skilled in implementing action proposals, and one by the pastor—which also was the one proposal that pastor insisted be in the committee's report.

As was pointed out in earlier pages, only rarely do standing committees become enthusiastic about implementing someone else's ideas. Standing committees naturally favor continuity. Most of the recommendations coming out of the typical special ad hoc study committee encourage discontinuity, change, and innovation. One of the standard functions of a standing committee is to be a cemetery for new ideas.

If all the recommendations coming from the long-range planning committee are directed solely at improving the quality of what is now being done, an argument can be made that standing committees can and will do that. If, however, the recommendations include major changes, it probably is unrealistic to refer those to a standing committee of volunteers for implementation. Thus a recommendation to increase the level of member contributions by 5 percent could be sent to the stewardship committee for implementation. By contrast, a recommendation to raise $200,000 to renovate the building probably will require the efforts of a special ad hoc action committee. Likewise a recommendation for patching that leaky roof could be sent to the trustees, but a recommendation to construct a large addition to the present building will best be accomplished by an ad hoc action committee.

A third alternative is for that special planning committee to disband on the assumption the governing board, not a set of standing committees, will implement the recommendations. Unless the majority of the members of that governing board perceive the existence of a crisis *and agree on the nature of the crisis,* that expectation usually turns out to be somewhere between naive and unrealistic. In most congregations the governing board already has a full agenda in responding to the month-by-month concerns. Only in small churches is it realistic to expect the governing board to formulate policy and also serve as an ad hoc action group.

The fourth alternative is the one suggested by Ronnie Brown. That is for the long-range planning committee to continue to meet and to accept responsibility for making sure all the recommendations at least receive a fair hearing.

In some churches that may be an acceptable compromise, but frequently it is less than the best course of action. Too often that committee does not possess the authority necessary for implementation of specific proposals. Often the criteria for selecting the membership of an ad hoc study committee are not the same qualifications one seeks in the membership of an ad hoc action committee. In many cases the members of the planning committee feel they have fulfilled their obligation when they forward their recommendations to the governing board.

If this is the road to be taken, it would be wise to decide that in advance, to include the authority to study *and to act* in the original charge to the committee, to take that dual role into consideration in establishing the criteria for selection of the members and, perhaps, to create a larger committee with one group responsible for the planning and an overlapping group concentrating on all stages of the implementation process. This option also is more likely to produce the desired results if the futures committee begins with a single issue agenda. If it is responsible for preparing a multi-faceted grand design (see chapter 3), it is unrealistic to expect that it also will be an effective implementation group.

The Best Choice

Frequently the best alternative is the one chosen intuitively by literally thousands of congregations. A common example is the growing congregation that needs more space. A study committee is created to recommend a specific course of action. After their recommendations have been submitted, two new ad hoc committees are appointed. The charge to one is to implement a construction and/or renovation program. The charge to the other is to design and implement a strategy to raise the money to pay for it.

A second example is the appointment of a special planning committee to examine staff needs. After those recommendations are received, discussed, perhaps amended, and adopted, three action committees may be appointed. The first is to meet with that staff member who is disappointed to discover his or her position is being eliminated and to arrange the timing and terms for the termination of that individual's employment. A second committee works with the pastor in recruiting, interviewing, and selecting the person(s) who are being considered to fill the new staff position(s) that will be created as a result of the study process. A third committee may be asked to secure the financial resources necessary for an expanded staff and program.

Perhaps the one crucial point in this discussion is that if the long-range planning committee will be expected to be responsible for the implementation of any recommendations it produces, that should be clearly and precisely stated in the motion to create it.

As a general policy, however, it often is wiser to appoint an ad hoc study committee with the responsibility for doing the planning and to create one or more ad hoc action committees to implement the resulting recommendations. (One example of that process is described in the next chapter.)

The most common exception to that generalization is when the ad hoc study or futures committee is given a narrowly and precisely defined assignment. This might be to choose a site for the future relocation of the meeting place or to design a church growth strategy or to expand the adult Sunday school or to investigate the possibility of creating a Mothers' Club or to study the possibility of a Wednesday after-school program for elementary school age children. If the subsequent recommendations do not produce the reaction that someone else's turf is being invaded and will not seriously disrupt the status quo, an argument can be made that the ad hoc committee should be asked to implement its own recommendations.

If, however, that study process produces several recommendations requiring substantial changes in the status quo, it may be wiser to ask new ad hoc action committees to accept the responsibility for implementation. That raises one of the most important issues to be examined in this whole book—and requires another chapter.

CHAPTER TWELVE

Implementing the Plan

ONE OF THE CHARACTERISTICS OF THE NEW TESTAMENT churches was their attraction for people filled with hope, daring, and the power of the Spirit.[1] This theme of hope for a better tomorrow also is central to the activities and teachings of the great reformers such as Martin Luther, Huldreich Zwingli, and John Wesley. The austere John Calvin, sometimes described as "the God-intoxicated" theologian, offered a strong note of hope in his doctrine of creation.[2] Hope is one of the central threads of the Heidelberg Catechism. Hope was and is one of the themes of the best known evangelists of the nineteenth and twentieth centuries. The hope derived from their belief in God is the force that produced the modern nation of Israel. Hope in the future is what motivates the farmer in the spring planting season following a summer marked by a severe drought. The New Testament teaches that God is the author and the source of hope (Rom. 15:13). Hope for a better tomorrow is the motivating force that has brought millions of immigrants to the shores of North America. When hope for a better tomorrow was unleashed in eastern Europe, in late 1989 and early 1990, it brought unbelievably rapid changes.

This theme of hope is the central organizing principle for thousands of Christian churches. This can be seen with remarkable clarity in the preaching, the singing, and the teaching of many of the congregations organized to reach the recent immigrants from Asia. This spirit of hope fills the air in the churches that are reaching the new generations of churchgoers born after 1955.

Hope, not institutional survival, should be the central motivating force that guides the deliberations of your long-range planning committee. Hope is the key to the implementation of that plan. Hope is the foundation for the vision that inspires people to act.

Hope plus vision plus planning plus leadership are the four critical ingredients for implementation of the recommendations of that futures committee.

What Happens Next?

The fifteen-page report from the long-range planning committee has been reproduced and submitted to the governing board of your congregation. It is universally understood that this completes the obligations of this seven-member team that has been meeting regularly for the past eight months. If the recommendations call for only modest changes, it may be feasible to delegate these to standing committees, but that is not true for this report. This report consists of four recommendations, each calling for substantial changes. The first recommendation calls for the creation of a package of new ministries designed to reach, attract, and serve families with young children. The second calls for a revision of the Sunday morning schedule with the addition of an early worship service preceding Sunday school and the creation of a second adult choir. The third recommendation identifies a new staff position for a person who will initiate and oversee that package of weekday ministries. The fourth recommendation calls for a $300,000 capital funds campaign to pay for the necessary renovation of the building, the demolition of the old parsonage that now serves as a parish hall, the construction of a one-story general purpose room on that site, and the paving of the gravel parking lot.

Ideally, all four recommendations are based on a carefully articulated vision of a new tomorrow for this congregation that inspires hope, optimism, and support for the detailed recommendations. Ideally, no one on the church council is surprised or dismayed when they read the final report. The regular and full communication between the long-range planning committee and the church council has created a sense of confidence, expectancy, hope, and enthusiastic support among the members of that governing board.

Two weeks following submission of the final report, an all-day retreat is held that includes all members of the governing board, the long-range planning committee, and the trustees, plus the chairpersons of all standing committees. The date for this retreat had been set back when the planning committee decided on the date for the submission of their printed report. This gave everyone a chance to reserve that date. Circulation of the final report for two weeks in advance gave everyone a chance to read it, reflect on it, discuss it with their friends, and prepare their questions. Those regular progress reports from the committee to the entire congregation via the parish newsletter plus two special mailings plus the widespread informal "corridor conversations" had eliminated the problem of negative responses to big surprises.

The chairperson of the church council presided at this all-day retreat. Following a carefully planned period of prayer and a discussion of three different New Testament images of the church, this chairperson suggested the recommendations from the long-range planning committee be divided in two categories. The first consisted of the proposed two new initiatives in ministry, the weekday program, and the expanded Sunday morning schedule. The second category included the means-to-an-end issues of additional staff, a capital funds campaign, and the construction program.

By four o'clock this collection of twenty-nine leaders had agreed (1) to appoint an ad hoc action committee, with authority to act, to begin the process of designing that new package of weekday programs and also to begin the search for a three-quarter-time staff person to create and direct this specialized ministry, (2) to appoint an ad hoc action committee to be chaired by the pastor to design an expanded Sunday morning schedule and with the authority to recruit someone to organize and direct that new adult vocal choir, but with the reservation that the proposed Sunday morning schedule would have to be submitted to the Church Council for approval before a date could be set for launching that new schedule, (3) to appoint a special capital funds committee to raise that $300,000, (4) to ask the trustees to begin the process of securing bids for demolition of the parish hall, (5) to appoint a building planning committee to begin the process of designing a new general purpose building and to investigate any necessary renovations of the forty-one-year-old church building, and (6) to postpone consideration of paving that gravel parking lot until after the construction had been completed.

This congregation's constitution calls for the church council to select the membership of all ad hoc committees. (The members of standing committees are nominated by a nominating committee and elected at the annual meeting.) Two members from that long-range planning committee agreed to serve on the seven-member action committee to design the new weekday program, one agreed to serve on the schedule committee, a fourth agreed to serve on the capital funds committee, and a fifth agreed to serve on the building planning committee. A sixth was in her second year as a trustee and continued in that role. When asked where he wanted to serve, the seventh member of the planning committee replied, "No, thanks, I'm tired and I'm not ready for any new volunteer responsibilities."

Out of the twenty-eight people who eventually agreed to serve on those four new action committees, eleven came from among those present at that all-day retreat and seventeen were not among the attenders. Ideally, that all-day retreat might have drawn as many as sixty or seventy people and eighteen to twenty of the members of these four action committees would have been present. That was not a serious problem, but it did mean more time at the first meeting of each action group was spent on "bringing everyone up to speed."

What Did They Do?

Following the creation of these four action committees, the pastor called together the three other chairpersons and offered this advice.

"Although it may appear these four committees have four different assignments, we actually have much in common. First of all, we worship the same God in the same building with the same people. While we have four different assignments, we are part of the same team. Second, the only safe assumption is that none of us has the support necessary to implement our assignment. Therefore each committee has to build its own support group. Third, while our long-range planning committee did an excellent job of keeping our members informed of their progress, that job is far from complete. The four of us need to meet together once a month just so we can keep up to date on the progress of what we're each doing. In addition, each committee should plan a once-a-month report for our weekly newsletter. That means every issue will include a report from one of these four action committees.

"Fourth," continued the pastor, "we need to stay in touch as we enlist allies so we don't overload the same volunteers. Fifth, the only safe assumption is the congregation as a whole is not ready to implement any of these recommendations, so we need to be selling our program to the people."

"Hold it, Pastor," interrupted the person chairing the action committee to design the new weekday program, "I thought the church council had approved all of this and the retreat was simply to move to the implementation stage. Are you telling us we still need congregational approval before we can do anything?"

"No and yes," replied the pastor. "No, we do not need congregational approval in a formal sense of a congregational vote. Approval of the church council is all we legally need, and we have that. What we must have, however, is as much support as we can muster from every member. We also must seek to minimize any opposition, hurt feelings, apathy, indifference, or resistance. That is what I mean by selling what we're doing."

"I guess that means both your committee and mine have to sell the people on change," commented the person chairing the building planning committee. "Your job is to change the schedule, and ours is to change the real estate."

"That's partially true," agreed the pastor, "but that is not the beginning point. The beginning point for all four is a combination of continuity, hope, tradition, faithfulness, and evangelistic outreach. If you read the report of the long-range planning committee, you saw the first three pages were devoted to an affirmation of the traditions of this congregation, to enthusiastic and optimistic statements of the expanded ministry God is calling this congregation to undertake from this historic location, to the continuity with the past when this church was organized back in 1948 to reach and serve families with young children, and to Jesus' call for us to go out and win new disciples. While we're all charged with initiating changes, we can accomplish that best by affirming the past and by relating what we're doing to the traditions of this parish."

"That sounds good," interrupted the person chairing the capital funds campaign, "but this congregation has never raised as much as $300,000 in one financial campaign before. Several of my friends already have told me that it can't be done. Tell me how this will be consistent with our local traditions."

"That's easy," smiled the pastor. "How much is $300,000? Roughly speaking, $300,000 is seventeen times the per capita personal income of the average resident of the United States today. Back in 1953 this congregation raised $60,000 in a two-year building fund campaign. How much was $60,000 in 1953? That was nearly forty times the per capita personal income of the American population in 1953. What we're proposing is in that same tradition of asking today's members to sacrifice on behalf of tomorrow's members, except this time we're asking for a more modest sacrifice. The members of 1953 sacrificed so we could enjoy this building today. We're asking today's members to sacrifice on behalf of a new generation of future members."

"I'm not as confident as you are that we have all the people behind this," questioned the person chairing the building planning committee. "I would be a lot more comfortable if we had a congregational meeting and got an affirmative vote of confidence from all the people before we do any more."

"That's a good point," conceded the pastor, "and we will have three or four votes on this whole plan. They won't be in the form you suggest, however. What we want are informed votes from people who can see the choices before us and who vote by their actions. Raising a hand to vote yea or nay is too easy. We want more meaningful votes. The way it now appears, the first vote will come on the first Sunday in September when we ask people to vote on a new schedule. Some will vote to come to the early service, others will vote to come to the late service, and I expect a few will stay away from both. Last year our attendance on the first Sunday in September was 169. I'm hoping that the combined attendance when we begin the two-service format will be at least two hundred. I will interpret that as a vote of approval.

"Our second vote," continued the pastor, "will come on the motion to raise $300,000. That motion was made and seconded at our retreat and our people will be asked to vote on it. Votes are a dollar apiece and anyone can vote as often as he or she wants. I expect we'll get over 300,000 yes votes on that one.

"Our third vote will come when we count the number of new people who participate in our weekday programming. That election won't be held for awhile, but in that one, people we have yet to meet will cast the decisive votes.

"Finally, our constitution does require a congregational meeting to approve any plans for major construction and I trust our building planning committee will bring in a plan that will win broad support at that meeting. So, our people will have several chances to vote on this whole program, but the most critical votes will be cast by people we have yet to meet, and they won't show up to vote unless all four of our committees get busy and complete our assignments."

A similar format may be useful in your church as you seek to implement the recommendations of your long-range planning committee.

The Influence of Momentum

For some other congregations, however, a different implementation strategy may be appropriate. One example of this is in the congregation in which every trend line has been down for the past several years. This includes declining attendance in both worship and Sunday school plus other cuts that undermine morale.

For these churches the first priority may be on producing a measurable, visible, affirming, and significant congregational victory. This might be in the form of organizing a new adult Sunday school class, or paying off that mortgage or painting the building or creating a new circle for younger women in the women's organization or doubling the enrollment in the Vacation Bible School or organizing a second vocal choir.

Before undertaking the implementation of a multi-faceted set of recommendations, it may be wise to produce one or two victories. This can raise the level of congregational self-esteem, create positive momentum, offer a cause for celebration, and provide a positive base for future action. It is easier to respond to a new challenge following a victory than it is to rally people following a defeat.

Overcoming Resistance

Finally, in many congregations any proposal for change will be met by resistance. Frequently this resistance is offered by only a minority of members, but they are articulate, persistent, negative, obstinate, and committed to the status quo. What can be done to overcome this resistance?

For many pastors the most attractive response is to take the advice of Jesus (Matt. 10:14), shake the dust from one's sandals, and move on to where the people will be more responsive.

A more creative alternative is to recognize the attachment to yesterday and the resistance to change as normal, natural, and predictable human behavior. This may mean winning the personal trust and confidence of the resisters *before* presenting proposals for change. Or it may mean enlisting allies for that new vision from among the spouses, adult children, parents, or close friends of the resisters. It often means giving people adequate time to talk themselves into supporting the dream, or at least moving to a position of neutrality.

Winning the support of the opposition may require compromises. It almost always requires more time, talk, persistence, delay, meetings, active listening, and the adjustment of priorities than the most enthusiastic proponents of immediate action believe to be realistic or necessary. It means accepting the fact that a voluntary organization usually needs a consensus, not simply a majority vote, to implement what some will perceive to be radical changes.

Occasionally, the situation will call for a new set of players if the goal is a new and different game. Operationally this may mean waiting for that day when it will be appropriate to replace two or three individuals who hold pivotal volunteer leadership positions. In other churches the essential changes may be impossible until fifty or a hundred new members come in with a new vision of what tomorrow could be in this place. Both strategies require patience. In other churches everyone is convinced that nothing can happen until after the present pastor retires and is succeeded by a more venturesome and creative minister. In a few churches no one is willing to undertake any new ventures in ministry until the size of that oppressive mortgage has been reduced. A capital funds appeal may be the best tactic for eroding that source of resistance.

Skilled and effective leaders recognize that overcoming resistance is a standard price to pay for change. Impatient activists have difficulty accepting that as normative.

When translated into a strategy for implementation, this means that every ad hoc action committee should include one or two exceptionally wise individuals who possess that intuitive gift for understanding what will be required in this time and place to overcome that natural, normal, and predictable resistance. With their help, the implementation process will be smoother!

NOTES

INTRODUCTION

1. Neil Postman, *Amusing Ourselves to Death* (New York: Penguin Books, 1985), pp. 36-63.

CHAPTER 1

1. Robert A. Walker, *The Planning Function in Urban Government* (Chicago: University of Chicago Press, 1950). For a pair of contrasting views on the place of planning in an organization, see John Stuart Mill, *On Liberty and Considerations on Representative Government* (Oxford: Basil Blackwell, 1948), p. 161, and Pierre Clavel, *The Progressive City* (New Brunswick, N.J.: Rutgers University Press, 1986), pp. 65-95.

2. While this will disturb some readers, much can be learned from the research conducted on military organizations. For example, those who despair over the inability of a large Protestant denomination, such as The United Methodist Church, to prepare and implement a strategic plan may be enlightened by reading Richard A. Gabriel, *Military Incompetence* (New York: Noonday Press, 1985), pp. 3-34. The primary barrier is in the institution, not in the people staffing that institution.

CHAPTER 2

1. An excellent book on contemporary teenagers is Francis A. J. Ianni, *The Search for Structure: A Report on American Youth Today* (New York: Free Press, 1989).

2. Robert E. Kelley, "In Praise of Followers," *Harvard Business Review*, November-December 1988, pp. 142-48.

3. Clark Kerr, *The Uses of the University*, 3rd ed. (Cambridge, Ma.: Harvard University Press), p. 177.

4. An explanation of this generalization can be found in Lyle E Schaller, *Getting Things Done* (Nashville: Abingdon Press, 1986), chapter 5.

CHAPTER 3

1. For another version of a pastor's grand design, see Lyle E. Schaller, *The Senior Minister* (Nashviile: Abingdon Press, 1988), pp. 29-38.

2. This distinction between a religious community and a business is described in greater detail in Lyle E. Schaller, *Looking in the Mirror* (Nashville: Abingdon Press, 1984), pp. 38-58.

CHAPTER 4

1. A discussion of the planning-from-strength model can be found in Lyle E. Schaller, *Effective Church Planning* (Nashville: Abingdon Press, 1979), pp. 93-110.

2. The use of the budget as a planning model is described in Lyle E. Schaller, *Parish Planning* (Nashville: Abingdon Press, 1971), pp. 36-63.

3. Several planning models for church growth are offered in Lyle E. Schaller, *Growing Plans* (Nashville: Abingdon Press, 1983), pp. 15-120.

4. A discussion of the future of the downtown church can be found in Lyle E. Schaller, *Choices for Churches* (Nashville: Abingdon Press, 1990), pp. 129-47.

5. The relationship of the small town rural church and the neighboring city churches is reviewed in *Choices for Churches*, pp. 149-79.

6. The dynamics of relocation are discussed in *Choices for Churches*, pp. 97-121.

7. Suggestions on resolving that financial crisis can be found in Lyle E. Schaller, *44 Ways to Expand the Financial Base of Your Congregation* (Nashville: Abingdon Press, 1989).

8. Suggestions for reversing that attendance decline can be found in Lyle E. Schaller, *44 Ways to Increase Church Attendance* (Nashville: Abingdon Press, 1988).

9. A discussion of the need to redefine roles can be found in Lyle E. Schaller, *Activating the Passive Church* (Nashville: Abingdon Press, 1981), pp. 40-120.

10. For a set of additional subjective questions on type, role, purpose, and style of ministry, see Lyle E. Schaller, *Looking in the Mirror* (Nashville: Abingdon Press, 1984), pp. 14-27, 59-200.

11. This paragraph is based on research contained in a fascinating book by Georges Ifrah, *From One to Zero: A Universal History of Numbers* (New York: Viking/Penguin, 1985).

12. Ibid., p. 10.

13. For a carefully documented analysis of the erosion of denominational loyalties, see Robert Wuthnow, *The Restructuring of American Religions* (Princeton, N.J.: Princeton University Press, 1988), pp. 71-99. See also George Gallup, Jr., and Jim Castelli, *The People's Religion: American Faith in the 90's* (New York: Macmillan Publishing Co., 1989), pp. 92-131, and Robert Wuthnow, *The Struggle for America's Soul* (Grand Rapids, Mich.: William B. Eerdmans Publishing Co., 1989).

14. For a discussion of twenty different models of racially integrated churches, see Lyle E. Schaller, "Whatever Happened to the Racial Integration of the Churches?" *Net Results,* October 1989, pp. 3-6.

15. This issue of central organizing principles is explored in greater depth in Schaller, *Choices for Churches,* pp. 13-72.

16. For a more detailed discussion of the potentialities of relocation, see *Choices for Churches,* pp. 97-121.

CHAPTER 5

1. Andrew M. Greeley, *Religious Change in America* (Cambridge, Mass.: Harvard University Press, 1989), p. 34.

2. David Hackett Fischer, *Albion's Seed* (New York: Oxford University Press, 1989), p. 423.

3. An exceptionally revealing analysis of the changes in rural churches can be found in Edward W. Hassinger, John S. Holik, and J. Kenneth Benson, *The Rural Church* (Nashville: Abingdon Press, 1988).

4. For a discussion of generational theory and its usefulness to long-range planning committees, see Lyle E. Schaller, *Reflections of a Contrarian* (Nashville: Abingdon Press, 1989), pp. 65-95.

5. A provocative book for those interested in the impact of television on preaching is Neil Postman's description of the "typographic mind" in *Amusing Ourselves to Death* (New York: Penguin Books, 1985), pp. 30-63.

6. A more extensive discussion of the impact of space on the life and ministry of a worshiping community can be found in Lyle E. Schaller, *Effective Church Planning* (Nashville: Abingdon Press, 1979), pp. 65-92, and Schaller, *Reflections of a Contrarian*, pp. 109-22.

7. Suggestions on this subject can be found in Lyle E. Schaller, *The Assimilation of New Members* (Nashville: Abingdon Press, 1987).

8. See Schaller, *Reflections of a Contrarian*, pp. 65-95.

9. A simple and lucid introduction to family systems theory is Michael E. Kerr, "Chronic Anxiety and Defining a Self," *The Atlantic Monthly*, September 1988, pp. 35-58.

10. For a brief discussion of the staff-to-size ratio, see Lyle E. Schaller, *The Multiple Staff and the Larger Church* (Nashville: Abingdon Press, 1980), pp. 51-84.

CHAPTER 7

1. Martin E. Marty, Stuart E. Rosenberg, and Andrew M. Greeley, *What Do We Believe?* (New York: Meredith Press, 1968), pp. 304-5.

2. The place of religion in the lives of the early immigrants from Britain is recounted in David Hackett Rischer, *Albion's Seed* (New York: Oxford University Press, 1989).

3. Ray Oldenburg, *The Great Good Place* (New York: Paragon House, 1989).

4. While not stated in these terms, this conflict between doing and being is discussed in a superb essay by Susan Harrington Devogel, "Clergy Morale: The Ups and Downs," *The Christian Century*, December 17, 1986, pp. 1149-52.

5. Marty, et al., *What Do We Believe?* pp. 304-5.

6. This contemporary migration of people across faith and denominational barriers is described in Robert Wuthnow, *The Restructuring of American Religion* (Princeton, N.J.: Princeton University Press, 1988); C. Kirk Hadaway, *What Can We Do About the Church Dropouts?* (Nashville: Abingdon Press, 1990); Andrew M. Greeley, *Religious Change in America* (Cambridge, Mass.: Harvard University Press, 1989); Randall Balmer, *Mine Eyes Have Seen the Glory* (New York: Oxford University Press, 1989); Ellen M. Rosenberg, *The Southern Baptists: A Subculture in Transition* (Knoxville: University of Tennessee Press, 1989); George Gallup, Jr., and Jim Castelli, *The People's Religion* (New York: Macmillan Publishing Co., 1989); Lyle E. Schaller, *It's a Different World!* (Nashville: Abingdon Press, 1987); and Robert Wuthnow, *The Struggle for America's Soul* (Grand Rapids, Mich.: William B. Eerdmans Publishing Co., 1989).

7. The inability of the Methodists, the Presbyterians, and other mainline denominations to reach the people born in the 1960s is described in Greeley, *Religious Change in America*, pp. 33-35. While 37 percent of the members, age 11 and over, of the Evangelical Lutheran Church in America were born before 1935, only 25 percent of the American population, age 11 and over, come from those age cohorts. *The Lutheran*, February 14, 1990, p. 25.

8. The concept of each parish functioning from a specific and clearly defined ideological stance is described in Joseph Hough, Jr., and Barbara G. Wheeler, eds., *Beyond Clericalism: The Congregation as a Focus for Theological Education* (Atlanta: Scholars Press, 1988). This might be satisfying to those seminary graduates who prefer the role of theologian-in-residence to the more complex role of pastor-preacher-administrator-leader-worship leader-teacher-trainer-model-of-a-committed-

Christian-evangelist-planner-prophet-and counselor. An excellent review of this book is Susan E. Schreiner, "Educating the Congregation," *The Christian Century*, November 1, 1989, pp. 985-87.

9. For a more detailed statement of this writer's position on building a parish's identity around ideology, see Lyle E. Schaller, *Looking in the Mirror* (Nashville: Abingdon Press, 1984), pp. 59-72, and Lyle E. Schaller, *Choices for Churches* (Nashville: Abingdon Press, 1990), pp. 47-49, 122-29, 171-74.

10. For two discussions on the highly divisive nature of pornography as an issue (especially among women), see Barry Sussman, *What Americans Really Think* (New York: Pantheon Books, 1988), p. 206, and the review essay by Alan Wolfe, "Dirt and Democracy," *The New Republic*, February 19, 1990, pp. 27-31.

11. The mutual incompatibility of the contemporary definitions of justice is discussed in James P. Sterba, "Recent Work on Alternative Conceptions of Justice," *American Philosophical Quarterly*, vol. 23, January 1986, pp. 1-22.

CHAPTER 8

1. For a description of some of the more common plateaus, see Lyle E. Schaller, *Looking in the Mirror* (Nashville: Abingdon Press, 1984), pp. 14-37.

2. For a longer discussion on church finances, see Lyle E. Schaller, *44 Ways to Expand the Financial Base of Your Congregation* (Nashville: Abingdon Press, 1989).

CHAPTER 9

1. Theodore Levitt, *Innovation in Marketing* (New York: McGraw-Hill, 1962)

2. Lyle E. Schaller, *44 Questions for Church Planters* (Nashville: Abingdon Press, 1991).

CHAPTER 12

1. Wayne A. Meeks, *The First Urban Christians* (New Haven: Yale University Press, 1983), pp. 190-92.

2. William J. Bouwsma, *John Calvin* (New York: Oxford University Press, 1988).